JUDGING JESUS

MAKING RIGHT JUDGEMENTS ABOUT WHAT TO BELIEVE

TOUGH QUESTIONS ANSWERED FOR THOSE WHO
HAVE BEEN ALIENATED FROM THE CHURCH

AND FOR THOSE WITHIN THE CHURCH WHO
HAVE UNMET NEEDS.

REV. JAMES P. MCCLAREY

Letters of Appreciation for the Work of Jim McClarey

Rev. McClarey's grasp of history, his understanding of semantics, and his sensitive approach to Bible Study has helped to deepen my faith, and to undergird my belief that the Bible is truly God's Word for us. Jana Waite.

Reverend James P. McClarey is a unique teacher of the Bible. He combines his in-depth expert knowledge of the Bible with a passion for teaching and understanding that only comes through Christ. Mike and Linda Barker.

Jim has an integrated approach to the Bible and is able to relate all parts of it to each other. That was something I needed even after 6 semesters of Bible Classes in a Christian College. He is never boring, and he lives what he believes. Kay McClarey

When he helps us understand the lesson, he shares his beliefs, but has always been respectful of our beliefs. Bill and Olive Getchius.

In Rev. McClarey's Bible studies, the isolated stories and events that I first learned as a child have been pulled together to form a firm foundation for my Christian faith. The result has been a much better understanding of the powerful and loving God we worship. Marilyn Hancock

Jim has an incredible knowledge of the Bible and a great insight into Bible times and how they relate to our lives and times. John Hancock.

He has such a wonderful way of bringing the Bible to life. His great knowledge of the Bible allows him to illustrate the background and lay the foundation for the different passages in the Bible. Gene and Roberta Johnson.

This book is dedicated to the Glory of God
in Jesus Christ.

CONTENTS

FOREWORD

For quite a few years I have been asked: "When is your book going to be done?" There are several reasons for the long delay that are difficult to elucidate: there were illnesses of my own and others; the conviction that I needed to grow more in Christ; and the conviction that I should not, while serving churches full time, take time away from serving the people of the church.

In many ways, I have been writing this book my entire life. As a United Methodist Church pastor for over forty-five years, I preached hundreds of sermons and led dozens of Bible studies all for the purpose of bringing theology into clear focus as part of practical living for everyone.

About ten years ago, things began to happen that I could explain in no way other than that I was experiencing a definite call from God to write the book. Let me explain, I have among other tools of learning, a concordance of over two thousand pages. As I fought to find time and to focus, I found that locations in the book I needed to reach, would come out right to the page as I opened the concordance. I did not have this happen by skill; I'm not that good. I kept records of all this and I have a desk drawer full of them. Often when I needed encouragement and wondered if God had given up on me, it would happen.

Now by the grace of God I believe the time has come. Not that I have fully arrived, growth in grace is always possible because of all that God has to give. I have been helped not only by events that were tinged with the special touch of God's "hand," but also by several people who believed in the need for it. In humility and gratitude, I want to thank them all. My daughter Jan Haggerty and my son Jim McClarey both played key roles; they know that I am forever beholden to each of them for taking responsibility for this project while they were both busy with their own lives. My granddaughter Sarah McClarey helped a great deal early on while I was learning to use a computer at age seventy-two, but she also offered insightful comments about the subject matter. Several others are mentioned in the pages of the book, such as Don and Elsie Westerman. I have not mentioned by name some people who have contributed to this book by being part of Bible study groups or discussions or by giving helpful advice. You know who you are, and you have my gratitude.

My dear wife, Kay McClarey, passed away during the writing of this book, but her support and influence must be recognized. Although the title

"Reverend" technically applied to me, Kay and I always had a joint ministry. She was active in volunteer leadership in all the local churches we served and made important contributions at the regional level. In our last move, we together started a chapel service at our home in Primrose Retirement Community. She took the writing of *Judging Jesus* seriously, contributed to lively discussions about its content, and supported me throughout the process. Together we achieved a state of oneness in our marriage. For all of that I remain in her debt.

INTRODUCTION

I said, "Mort, if the Christian faith had been presented to me the way it was to you, I wouldn't be a Christian either."

Mort was surprised to hear that from a pastor. But he felt affirmed. He said, "Maybe there is another way to look at it." Then he began to explore matters of faith all over again.

It started early in my ministry. I began to meet a lot of people like Mort, both in and out of church, who struggled with their faith. They had encountered particularly difficult life circumstances, or they had deep searching questions that were not being answered. As a pastor I made it a large portion of my lifelong work to find answers for the people with the toughest questions.

Years ago, Mort and I had time for a very long talk when there was a bad ice storm in our small Illinois town. Mort and his wife Kay had lost electrical power, leaving them stranded with no heat in the dead of winter. My wife (also named Kay) and I invited them to stay with us in our home until their power was restored. This took several days, during which Mort saw that we were real people, excusing ourselves to take care of our baby daughter, preparing food, and so on. I became less and less "the preacher" to him, and he began to share the things that were bothering him about Christianity as it had been taught to him.

Mort's sentiments ran as follows: "They say that if I just believe strongly enough, that I will have no more problems. But I don't see the Christians being any better off in their health or family issues. I hear preachers promising wealth to people who accept Jesus. They make sure to attract plenty of income while they make these claims. That turns me off totally. They say that God is all love, but when I read the Bible for myself I find stories of God striking people with awful diseases. Even God demanding that people be killed for simply being in the way of the so-called Promised Land. This does not seem very loving to me; yet when I question it, I am told I am disrespecting Holy Scripture that I should 'just have faith' in the Bible.

"They say that God never changes, but they also say that God doesn't do healing miracles any more. Which is it? How can I put my trust in something that is so unclear?

"Really Jim, you are an educated man; how do you support these Christian teachings?", Mort wanted to know.

As I listened to him talk about what he had been told, I thought to myself, "No wonder he doesn't believe." That is why I told him that if the Christian faith had been presented to me the way it had been to him, I would not have believed it either.

Mort and I became friends during that ice storm, and he began to re-examine matters of faith. In time, Mort accepted Jesus as his Lord and Savior. But not before many of his legitimate questions were answered.

If you have ever felt you were being asked to give up your intellect in order to keep your faith, this book is for you. These pages are for people who are trying to solve faith intellectually and people with other problems. It is my heartfelt prayer that in the pages ahead, God will greatly bless you wherever you most need it now.

JUDGING OUR FAITH IN TIMES OF CRISIS

As a pastor, I have encountered many people shaken in their faith. Enduring struggles with such things as addictions, or financial stress caused them to question their beliefs. Over the decades, members of my churches also talked with me about broken relationships, broken promises, broken dreams, loneliness. . . Having a strong belief system is no guarantee that life will be free of pain or loss. But when our faith has been clarified and proven by truth, it can be a source of strength in times of grief. I know. I, too, have suffered.

When I was a young man, my wife Kay gave birth to our third child, Jeanie. It was a dangerous birth, and Kay nearly bled to death. Let me tell you the story.

Back in those days, husbands were relegated to waiting rooms instead of participating in the messes and joys of modern delivery rooms. So while my wife experienced labor surrounded by kind strangers, I waited alone in another room. I would have felt completely isolated if not for someone else in the room. A man named Dick sat just a few feet away while his wife Pat was also in labor.

Hours passed without news. Dick and I talked and felt the connection of our shared experience. Though the hour grew late, nervous-husband apprehension kept me fully awake. Finally a nurse came in. Dick and I stopped talking and both looked at her expectantly. "Mr. Tolker,[1] you have a daughter." She told him the baby's weight and then left. The room seemed to release a long-held breath. Dick grinned, and I congratulated him.

Not long after, the nurse returned. "Mr. McClarey, it's a girl. She weighs seven pounds."

Jeanie. Our second daughter.

Now I was the one smiling and being congratulated. Dick and I relaxed in our seats, thinking of our wives and our infant daughters.

Sometime later the nurse came back. She looked straight at me. "There was a complication during delivery. The umbilical cord was wrapped around the baby's neck, strangling her. We're trying to keep her breathing, but we're fighting against the odds." While I struggled to take that in, she added, "And Kay has lost a lot of blood. Her blood pressure is very low. Both situations are serious."

Minutes dragged by. The nurse returned again, this time to speak to Dick. Incredibly, she gave him the same update about his new daughter and his wife. That night, I was not "a pastor" to Dick. I was just another husband and father in pain, living my own nightmare alongside him. If my faith in God up to that point had caused me to believe I would be exempt from this kind of terror, I would certainly have begun to question God right there.

Our fears worsened with each slow tick of the wall clock.

Another hour passed, maybe two. Time became a blur. I didn't know if my daughter was going to live. I didn't know if my wife was going to make it.

After a long time, the nurse hurried in to tell Dick that his daughter and wife were all right. They would both live. Dick's head was still in his hands in gratitude when the nurse appeared in the doorway once more.

"Mr. McClarey, we lost your baby. We did everything we could."

I felt sunken. Despair. I'd kept control. Now I lost hold of it.

But the nurse had not finished relaying her news. "And your wife's blood pressure is still down around thirty. We're trying to keep her going."

By now I was so tired and so filled with grief that my thinking was not entirely clear. But if my understanding of God had been based on anything other than what Jesus said about God, I might very well have lost my faith that night.

At last, Kay began to recover. I went in to see her, feeling shaken yet wanting to help her in her trauma and grief. After the baby had died, the hospital staff had removed her, and Kay had never seen Jeanie. She kept telling the nurses, "I want to see my baby. I want to see my baby." Then Kay looked to me and said, "Why won't they let me see my baby? I want to see her!"

It is terrible to lose a child. All I knew to tell her was what the professionals had told me, "The doctors think that wouldn't be best for you, that seeing the baby would make losing her even harder." It was not my best moment, but that was decades ago, and psychology has advanced since then. I could only do what I thought best at the time. I have rarely experienced such a terrible sense of helplessness.

For both Kay and me, recovery would be long in coming. While I was grieving the death of our baby daughter Jeanie and simultaneously watching my wife's anguish, I could relate to those who say, "If God is so powerful, why then does God allow the innocent to suffer? Perhaps God is not really God, or God is not relevant for today."

Perhaps you have suffered through a nightmare of your own but without the benefit of a seasoned faith in a God you could trust with your breaking heart. As long as I live (and Jeanie would be over 50 years old now), I will never forget the darkness or the pain or the fear of losing a child and nearly losing my young wife. That experience has made me a pastor who understands severe pain and loss. I have sat beside many hurting people, and I know that quoting Bible verses is not always helpful in those situations.

The answers are there in the Bible, but not necessarily in convenient packages to leave unopened until needed. If you, like my friend Mort, have felt the Bible to be unreliable during times of trouble, this book is for you. Please don't wait until you are in the middle of trauma to make judgments about the validity of your own faith in God.

The earliest Christians faced difficulties, too. In fact, their troubles often got much worse after they were known to be believers in "the Way", as Christianity was called at first. Why did they hold onto faith in Jesus Christ during personal trials? The short answer is that they evaluated the claims of Jesus against what they knew from scripture, found the claims to be true, and staked their entire lives on that truth. Once a person determined that Jesus was indeed the Christ (Messiah) promised in scripture, she or he began to re-evaluate those same scriptures in light of Jesus' teachings. This process plays out before us in the New Testament.

In politics and in business, we use a sometimes messy process called "vetting". We try to uncover all the truth, whether positive or negative. We hope that a thoroughly vetted candidate will be able to withstand unforeseen pressures later on when in the role of elected official or business manager. So we do the work of vetting before we approve a candidate. Whether or not we realize it, we are judging the person.

Do not be afraid to judge the claims of Jesus Christ for yourself. A thorough "vetting" of Jesus Christ and your reasons for faith will result in a stronger faith that will hold true in times of trouble. If this disturbs you, note that Jesus asked, "Do you not yet understand?" to several groups and individuals. See Mark 4:13, Mark 8:21, and John 3:10 for some examples.

Look at the conversation between Jesus and Nicodemus described in John 3:1-21 (NRSV)[2]. This religious leader, afraid to be seen with Jesus, nonetheless wanted to know whether Jesus might be telling the truth. He came alone at night and twice asked, "how can this be?" Jesus responded with answers, not scolding. In fact, this very setting contains the most famous Bible verse of them all:

"For God so loved the world that he gave his only Son, so that everyone who believes in him may not perish but may have eternal life." John 3:16

"Okay, I will try to 'judge Jesus,'" you say, "But isn't that wrong? Didn't Jesus say, 'Do *not* judge'?" (Matthew 7:1) Yes, he did but in the context of our relationships with other people.

Jesus also said, "Make right judgements," in contexts of teaching what to believe. (See Luke 12:57 and John 7:24.) Like Nicodemus and like my old friend Mort, you can judge correctly what to believe about Jesus and the Bible. I believe you will be rewarded with answers you can believe. And trust.

Maybe you have been told to spend more time reading the Bible, to "pray the Psalms" perhaps. Someone has told you that if you just believe every word in the Bible, and apply it, you will have all the answers you need. Well, let's try that. Open your Bible, and read Psalm 137, verse 9, "Happy shall they be who take your little ones and dash them against the rock!" How *could* I, as a father who has lost a baby, ever suggest that a hurting person should find comfort in this particular verse? Yet, there it is, right in the center of the Bible.

Yes, I have heard many true stories of people opening their Bibles randomly and finding pertinent answers and help for their souls. God is certainly able to guide us to exactly what we need. I have had that experience personally. But I also know people who tried the random approach and were disappointed or even shocked at what they found.

Some people are upset when any part of the Bible is questioned, believing that challenges undermine the authority of God's Holy Word. But if we do not ask the questions that are in our minds, we run the risk of never growing in our faith. My faith is strong, not simply because of my emotional fervency. And certainly not because of my refusal to entertain questions. Yet some people have taught that we should "just have faith" and have discouraged questioning. This is why I suggest that you familiarize yourself with the words that Jesus spoke by reading the New Testament first. Then when you go on to read the rest, you will be able to look at all scripture through the lens of what Jesus said about it. You will have a much deeper and more accurate understanding that is acceptable to your mind and satisfying to your soul.

I do believe that God is the loving and powerful God that Jesus proclaimed. In fact, I have staked my entire life on this truth, but not without having some of my most important questions answered. I don't want to imply here that we must have *every* question answered before we choose to believe. We will never get to the point where we know everything. In fact, throughout my life, I have continued to ask questions. My faith still grows when I do. On the other hand, I am so glad I learned enough in order to be confident in my faith before that awful time of losing Jeanie.

What Jesus Says Goes

In this book, I will show you several passages from the Old Testament. Know now that if there is apparent conflict between different parts of the Bible, *what Jesus says goes*. How can I be so confident about this? There is no greater place to start explaining than Hebrews chapter eight:

"But Jesus has now obtained a more excellent ministry, and to that degree he is the mediator of a better covenant, which has been enacted through better promises. For if that first covenant had been faultless, there would have been no need to look for a second one." Hebrews 8:6-7

Do not overlook this foundational statement in the New Testament. These two verses are quite plain. When you know that the words "covenant" and "testament" are interchangeable, you will be able to see that Jesus is the supreme interpreter of all scripture. In fact, Jesus is the Word of God "in flesh" or we would say today "in person." In any discussion about what is true in any part of the Bible, our deciding factor needs to be, "what did Jesus say or do about this?"

Look at Hebrews 8:6-7 in any of the widely used translations of the Bible and you will find the same thing. Whatever the choice of words, the essential meaning remains; the Old Testament is not without fault. This does not mean that the Old Testament is without merit. Reading the Old Testament after first building a strong understanding of the teaching and life of Jesus can spark great discussions and growth. Some of the crucial terms in the Hebrews passage are of measurement and comparison; "more" excellent, "to that degree", "better" covenant, "better" promises and "more excellent ministry." Hebrews 8:7 makes the bold assertion that the first Covenant/Testament has faults. Its limitations are not adequately glimpsed until the "more excellent ministry" of Jesus comes into light. The Christ is anticipated by the better side of the Old Testament.

A new covenant (or "testament") was needed.
The Book of Hebrews makes it clear that the New
Covenant is an Eternal one, while the Old Covenant,
laid out in the Old Testament was not. Another way
of saying this is that God was fully in Jesus' birth,
life, death, resurrection and continued living
presence in the Church as the Body of Christ. This is
laid out in chapters 3 through 7 of Hebrews. In these
chapters the Old Testament is said to be earth-based,
which means that the vision of God in it, while
positive in many of its parts, is not quite the full
vision of the God of the eternal "tent" or
"tabernacle."

If you feel that the words of Hebrews 8:6-7 as
shown here knock the props out from under you, be
assured that something better awaits you. According
to Hebrews 8:6 above, better promises are there for
you. Better promises have to do with better
prophecies. And these are the promises you can
stake your faith on. The "better prophesies of the
Old Covenant" are the ones that best fit the
teachings and actions of Jesus.

Some of the prophecies in the Old Testament do
mirror the teachings and actions of Jesus. However,
those that look forward to crushing enemies,
enjoying the spoils of war and the eventual ruling of
the world from Jerusalem are definitely different in

spirit and in application than Jesus' call to loving enemies and returning evil with good. Following his triumphal entry into Jerusalem and its Temple, Jesus said to the chief priests and elders of the people:

"Therefore I tell you, the Kingdom of God will be taken away from you and given to a people that produces the fruits of the kingdom." Matthew 21:43

The Old Testament sayings that do not mirror the Spirit of Jesus may be what the Apostle Paul had in mind when he said, "for we know only in part, and we prophesy only in part; but when the complete comes, the partial will come to an end." (I Corinthians 13:9) Then in I Corinthians 14 Paul begins to lay out a more mature understanding of prophecy. Prophecy entails both fore-telling (that is, predicting the future) and forth-telling (that is, commenting on God's will for God's people in a sort of editorial manner).

The Old Testament book of the Prophet Joel includes a great foreshadowing of a future visitation of the Spirit (which we call Pentecost). Here are the words of Joel 2:28-29, that *did* find a place in the New Testament:

"No, this is what was uttered through the prophet Joel: 'In the last days it will be, God declares, that I will pour out my spirit upon all flesh, your sons and your daughters shall prophesy, and your young men shall see visions, and your old men shall dream dreams. Even on my slaves, both men and women, in those days, I will pour out my spirit; and they shall prophesy.'" Acts 2:16-18

Peter, the speaker here and one of Jesus' disciples, recognized that the giving of the spirit to a wide number of Jewish believers gathered from many countries, was a fulfillment of the above prophecy of Joel. In Acts, the prophecy was not only being acted out at Pentecost, it also affirmed that Jesus was both Lord and Messiah. "Therefore let the entire house of Israel know with certainty that God has made him both Lord and Messiah, this Jesus whom you crucified." (Acts 2:36)

Yet this same Old Testament prophet also provides a classic example of the Zionist doctrine of Israel's domination of the world from Jerusalem in the end-time. In Joel 3, the Jews of the dispersion [3] are to be gathered from the nations that enslaved them, after which the people of Israel will be asked to "beat plowshares into swords and pruning-hooks into spears." (Joel 3:10) This is in direct contradiction to the more famous prophecies of Isaiah chapter 2 and Micah 4 that call for beating swords into plowshares and spears into pruning hooks.

Here we are faced with a dilemma. We can see that Joel 3 is in the Bible, and if we refuse to consider questions about its validity for today, we miss the fact that Jesus is more righteous and more powerful than the prophet Joel. Yet this is the approach some people have taken. They suggest closing our minds with the statement, "whatever is in the Bible I believe without question." When my friend Mort asked about things like Joel 3, he was unsatisfied with the "just have faith" answer. It seemed to him a glaring inconsistency, and he needed this tough question answered with logic. He wanted to believe, but as long as this passage was unexplained, he was suspicious that the Christian faith might not be able to stand up to valid criticism.

This illustrates just one example of what I said about the benefits of being very familiar with Jesus' teaching before trying to find comfort and guidance in the Old Testament. By reading the Old Testament in light of Jesus Christ's life and example, we can discern that this part of Joel is one of the passages that Jesus transcended.

When we grasp this duality between Christ-like teachings and those not true to the spirit of Christ within a single book as shown in Joel, we begin to understand the way the Bible records its visions. Out of respect for history, the Bible writers often laid

right beside each other contrasting visions. In the
case of Joel, the vision that led to Pentecost featured
the work of the Holy Spirit in bringing together as
one, old and young, male and female, slave and free.
But the writer also gave us the Zionist vision
mentioned above. I have long said of the Old
Testament that *Jesus embodied the best and
transcended the rest.*

Look at the Old Testament book of Leviticus
where in 26:18-33 God is characterized as
threatening to punish the people of Israel seven-fold
for their manifold sins. The picture painted in those
verses is frightening and gruesome to behold. Surely
this is a different concept of God than what Jesus
taught. The Way of Jesus is not the way of bearing
grudges and vicious retaliation. Judgment, yes.
Vicious retaliation, no.

And surely, it is the concept that Jesus taught that
we want to proclaim as the best, a truth we can trust.
Many discussions of the nature of "an eye for and
eye and a tooth and for tooth" overlook this view
from Leviticus that portrays God as not only
vindictive, but also as one who will punish people
by making them extremely ill. Leviticus even
advocates the murder of large groups of people,
often including their children.

The Old Testament prophet Jeremiah said of the future, "In those days they shall no longer say: 'The parents have eaten sour grapes, and the children's teeth are set on edge.' But all shall die for their own sins; the teeth of everyone who eats sour grapes shall be set on edge." (Jeremiah 31:29-30) This was immediately before he foretold the New Covenant. Jeremiah wrote years after Leviticus, so his prophesy shows growth and reflection happening during the years the Old Testament writings were being produced and preserved.

How appropriate that the writer of Hebrews quotes the prophecy of a New Covenant in 8:8-12. In Jeremiah it is found in 31:31-34. Though Jeremiah was projecting into the future, the words are in full agreement with the Hebrews description; the New Testament will not be like the Old. (8:9) It will be based on God's gift through forgiving grace and the gift of God's own spirit. (8:12) Its ultimate goal is that everyone will come to know God personally from the least of them to the greatest. (8:11) This calls to mind the beautiful expression of Isaiah: "The earth will be full of the knowledge of the Lord as the waters cover the sea." (Isaiah 11:9)

It also is similar in tone to a beautiful Psalm:

"The Lord is merciful and gracious, slow to anger and abounding in steadfast love. He will not always accuse, nor will he keep his anger forever. He does not deal with us according to our sins, nor repay us according to our iniquities. For as the heavens are high above the earth, so great is his steadfast love toward those who fear him; as far as the east is from the west, so far he removes our transgressions from us. As a father has compassion for his children, so the Lord has compassion for those who fear him. For he knows how we were made; he remembers that we are dust."
Psalm 103:8-14

The closing verse of Hebrews chapter 8 is even more emphatic in showing the greater value of the New Covenant in the words:

"In speaking of a 'new covenant', he has made the first one obsolete. And what is obsolete and growing old will soon disappear." Hebrews 8:13

To some this may seem revisionist in nature on the part of humans; not so, it is *the Lord* who makes this move.

There are critics of this way of handling the Old Testament who say things like, "Look. You snip a little bit here, and a little bit there," implying that you are directly taking something from God's Word, as if to say, "How dare anyone suggest that some of the Old Testament is at points not in line with the teachings of Jesus?"

However, the reverse is more apt. When you feel you have to accept the entire Old Testament as is, you snip not a little but a <u>lot</u> from the profile of Jesus Christ, the Living Word of God, who is the author of the better covenant! Since it is Jesus whose teachings and actions call for the snipping, we should follow in his steps.

I have to say that there is a widespread tendency to dodge the deep questions about the intent of much of the Old Testament laws. It may be a case of "letting sleeping dogs lie." If this is done knowingly, I would say that those who do so are guilty of de-facto disbelief. Mark Twain long ago raised the question: "Why do they (the pastors of churches he had attended) hide all the bad stuff?" [4] The question is still apt. How many thinking people in our day have pulled away from the entire Christian enterprise because they receive little help with their honest questions about the Bible?

I came to the conclusion long before I found sufficient backing for my viewpoint, that "fulfilling the Law and the Prophets" meant filling them full, or making them more complete. I also was quite sure that at some levels, the picturing of God as vindictive, sending disease at times instead of healing, and even advocating a kind of holy war mixed with ethnic cleansing needs to be changed, not just completed. I needed something beyond my own interpretation to cite. So I kept asking, believing that the answer would be given to me, seeking, that I might find, knocking, in hope that the door would be opened. *And then it happened.*

While shopping in a Christian Bookstore, one day, my eye fell on a Complete Jewish Bible that included the New Testament. It is written from the viewpoint of Jewish Christians. I began to read the Introduction, and the paragraph that began: DID YESHUA 'FILL' the TORAH? This is what I beheld:[5]

"The common Greek word *plerosai* means to 'fill.' At *Mattityahu* (Matthew) 5:17 most translators render it 'to fulfill'. My view is that Yeshua came not to 'fulfill, but to 'fill' the Torah and the ethnical pronouncements of the Prophets 'full' with their complete meaning so that all can know all that obedience entails."

Then the powerful paragraph adds the words: "In fact, this is the theme of the entire Sermon on the Mount." The final statement announces that, "When the Messiah comes he will both explain the obscure passages of Torah and actually change it."[6]

Coming from scholars with a strong background of respect for the Old Testament, as did this passage, this was the validation I needed. After finding it, I felt completely secure in my thinking about the words and actions of Jesus Christ actually overriding parts of the Old Testament.

So. Which parts?

The Great Law of Israel, the "Shemah, Shemah, Y'Israel" (hear, hear O Israel) might be thought to be the highest level of the Old Testament due to the fact that Jesus seemed to treat it that way in the famous interview with a wealthy young Lawyer. Upon examination there is yet another surprise that comes in looking up the Old Testament texts involved in the discussion.

The Great Law, the Shemah, Shemah, Y'Israel reads:

"Hear, O Israel: the Lord is our God, the Lord alone. You shall love the Lord your God with all your heart, and with all your soul, and with all your might."   Deuteronomy 6:4-5

Please notice especially that the words: "And your neighbor as yourself" are not in the above passage. Consequently they are not part of the Old

Testament Great Law, but this is not the main surprise. In Jesus' famous interchange with a certain lawyer in Luke 10:25-28, Jesus was asked, "What must I do to inherit eternal life?" Jesus turned the question on him, "What do you read? What is written in the law?" At that point the lawyer answers in the words of Deuteronomy 6:4-5, as printed above, and he added, *"and your neighbor as yourself."*

As Jesus knew, the law concerning love of neighbor is not from Deuteronomy, but from Leviticus 19:17-18. Here the neighbor is identified as "any one of *your* people;" in other words, people of Israel. This is Jesus "embracing" the Old Testament scripture and pushing it to a higher meaning, in other words "transcending."

How about Jesus' critique of the Old Testament as teaching hate of enemies? This is sometimes questioned. Surely God wouldn't hate. One need only turn to the last book of the Old Testament, in order to find a picture of the Lord as hating an enemy, Esau by name, and Edom, the people springing from Esau:

"I have loved you, says the Lord. But you say, "How have you loved us?" Is not Esau Jacob's brother? says the Lord? Yet I have loved Jacob, but I have hated Esau." Malachi 1:2-3a

Malachi goes on to picture the Lord as saying that anytime Edom rebuilds, God will tear her down. The Edomites are to be looked on as the people with whom God is angry forever. This is strange in light of the fact that Deuteronomy 23:7 reads, "You shall not abhor any of the Edomites, for they are your kin." This is an inconsistency that cannot simply be explained away. It is yet another example of the fact that the Old Covenant does not speak with one voice.

Jesus knew about the state of things in his time when he in Matthew 5:17 said that he came to complete "The Law and the Prophets." Since the New Testament holds that Jesus as the Messiah is the Living Word of God made flesh, Christ is thus the "canon" or "rule" that determines what is Christ-like in the writings we know as the Bible. This is huge and must not be passed over.

Remember that Jesus is the living word of God. Therefore, Jesus is the one who is in the position to determine what part of the New Covenant is greater than the old as we have seen in Hebrews 8:6-7 and Matthew 5:17-20.

It is natural to ask: "How can we tell what is and what is not worthy of Christ in the Old Testament?" Important question. One of the greatest keys to the way Jesus interpreted the Bible, is found in a quote of the Old Testament in the New: Isaiah 61:1-2 quoted in Luke 4:16-30.

In Luke 4:14 we hear of Jesus returning to Galilee from experiences in the wilderness and near Jerusalem. He was teaching in various synagogues and "was praised by everyone." As a man returning to his home town, he evidently was asked to read from the Book of the Prophet Isaiah.

He stood up to read what was either an assigned reading or one chosen by himself. He found the place where it was written:

"The Spirit of the Lord God is upon me, because the Lord has anointed me; he has sent me to bring good news to the oppressed, to bind up the brokenhearted, to proclaim liberty to the captives, and release to the prisoners; to proclaim the year of the Lord's favor." Isaiah 61:1-2

Turn to Isaiah 61:1-2 at this point, and notice that Jesus stopped reading in the middle of a sentence. What did he leave out? the parallel statement "and the day of vengeance of our God."

This omission speaks volumes. Jesus knew perfectly well that he stopped before the end of the passage.

The people of Nazareth were probably taken with the Zionist philosophy based on Numbers 34 and the boundaries that will (in the minds of the Zionists) be guaranteed, which included Israel's enemies being destroyed by God in "the year of the Lord's favor". They would have been quite happy with the inclusion of vengeance on the nations that had enslaved them. But Jesus did not see God as one who dealt in vengeance. Justice? Yes. Tough love? Yes. Vengeance? No.

Then Jesus sat down and said, "Today this scripture has been fulfilled in your hearing." (Luke 4:21) Among those who heard Jesus read that day, some would have noticed that Jesus left out the vengeance half of the verse from Isaiah, and some would not. Most could have missed his meaning in the statement afterward. They continued speaking well of his words and marveled that Joseph's son had come so far.

When we look back on that statement with the benefit of hindsight, we can see that Jesus used this opportunity to announce himself as God's anointed One. "Today this scripture has been fulfilled in your hearing." This would not have been obvious even to the disciples so early in the three years of Jesus' ministry on earth.

What followed after that, however, made the crowd so angry that they "drove him out of the town" and tried to throw him down a cliff. (Luke 4:29) Why the anger? Jesus gave some illustrations from the Old Testament that showed God cared for other nations, not *just* Israel. The prevailing thought at the time was that God loved the Israelites more than or even to the exclusion of the people of other nations. So Jesus' reminder that God showed favor to people outside of Israel made people angry enough to want him dead or at least out of town.

See Matthew 21:43. "Therefore I tell you, the kingdom of God will be taken away from you and given to a people that produces the fruits of the kingdom." Here, Jesus made it clear that if Israel did not fulfill its call to act in accordance with the call to bear the fruits of living appropriately to God's establishing the Kingdom of Heaven on earth, the Kingdom would be given to *another nation*. The seeming effrontery of Jesus was not without contextual relevance. He had come into the world to show a greater love than loving those who love you and hating your enemies.

Let us not ignore the Old Testament prophet Amos who punctured that kind of smug attitude long ago in his words in Amos:

"Are you not like the Ethiopians to me, O people of Israel? says the Lord. Did not I bring Israel up from the land of Egypt, and the Philistines from Caphtor and the Arameans from Kir? The eyes of the Lord God are upon the sinful kingdom, and I will destroy it from the face of the earth except that I will not utterly destroy the house of Jacob, says the Lord." Amos 9:7-8

My own dear wife Kay, who died during the writing of this book, was among those who preferred to read the New Testament mostly to the exclusion of the Old. However, in her mature years, she found much comfort in the better parts of the Old Testament. It is well to lift up a few inspiring and wonderful Old Testament passages lest we become tempted to throw out the entire collection.

Psalm 103 has a glowing sense of healing and grace that are out of proportion to any times of correction and punishment. Its sense of understanding provides a needed relief from the mistaken visions of God as petulant, controlling and given to vengeance.

Hosea 11 shows the tender care of God for the children of Israel as they journey from slavery in Egypt to a new start in the Land of Canaan. Despite the fact that Israel was unappreciative and rebellious at times, the Lord still cannot and will not follow up a temptation to have done with them.

Isaiah 6, so important to Jesus, gives us an inspiring account of Isaiah's worship in the temple in a time of great distress. Isaiah in chapters 42 and

49 shows that God has called Israel to be a light to the nations as over against concern only for itself, and thereby inspired Jesus to tell his hearers in the Beatitudes of Matthew chapter 5 that they are the Light of the World. Chapters 52 and 53 of Isaiah tell of the suffering love of God shown in and through an innocent sufferer that Jesus acted out to the ultimate degree, and the closing chapters of Isaiah abound with expressions of a New Heaven and a New Earth to come.

It has been said that the ancient Hebrews gave to the world the gift of hope. The beautiful Psalm 8, worshiping God through God's awesome universe, is tops. It expresses both the feeling of smallness in such a vast and impressive array of sun, moon, stars, and yet exults in the faith that God counts us as of great worth.

> [1] "O LORD, our Sovereign, how majestic is
>   your name in all the earth!
> You have set your glory about the heavens.
> [2] Out of the mouth of babies and infants
> you have founded a bulwark because of your
>   foes,
> to silence the enemy and the avenger.

3 When I look at your heavens, the work of
   your fingers, the moon and the stars, that
   you have established
4 What are human beings that you are mindful
   of them,
mortals that you care for them?
5 Yet you have made him a little lower than
   God, and crowned them with glory and
   honor. . .
9 O LORD, our Sovereign,
how majestic is your name in all the earth!"
   Psalm 8:1-5,9

The people of the Old Testament, in spite of low
points, were among the cultures that early in
recorded history began to protect widows and
children and those who were "down and out,"
wielding the force of Law. In this they furnished the
backdrop for Jesus' concern for the sick, the
impoverished, and those with no power. Those who
read the Book of Proverbs carefully will note a
concern for the poor throughout its pages. In fact,
several of the wisdom sayings of the book are very
much in accord with the spirit of Jesus.

This Jesus, who is greater than the Old
Testament prophets, is the one in whom I trusted

during the shock and sadness of losing our baby
daughter so long ago. I have continued trusting Jesus
throughout my life since then.

Regarding the Old Testament Scripture, Jesus
embodied the best and transcended the rest. After
all, though Jesus completed the Law and the
prophets, he said he did not come to destroy them. I
do not ask you to "just have faith" without having
some of your questions about disturbing passages in
the Old Testament answered. When you familiarize
yourself with the words that Jesus spoke, you will be
able to take comfort in the Psalms and many other
wonderful Old Testament passages.

You will be able to do this because you will
know Jesus is the supreme interpreter of all
scripture. Therefore, when you come across
upsetting passages, you can look at them through the
lens of what Jesus said and did. In this way, you will
be able to build a deep faith and an accurate
understanding that is acceptable to your mind and
satisfying to your soul.

JUDGING THE OLD TESTAMENT THROUGH JESUS

The story of the other dad in the hospital waiting room where I learned our baby had died in birth did not end when I left the scene. Dick and his wife Pat were part of a church in central Illinois. Thirteen years later, my wife and I were transferred to that church. By then, Kay and I felt we had gone as far as we could with the grieving and healing process after Jeanie's death. But seeing Dick and Pat's daughter Laurie, now a teenager, brought back strong feelings that surprised us. We wondered if our transfer there was a coincidence or part of God's unfolding plan for our lives. We soon began to trust that our meeting Dick, Pat, and Laurie again was a beautiful way God moved to help us heal more fully from the pain of losing a child.

Laurie was wheelchair bound and had challenges related to the brain being deprived of oxygen during her difficult birth. Dick and Pat never stopped being grateful that their daughter's life was spared that terrible night. Still, that night was the beginning of years of specialized medical treatments and special education and special food and special equipment. They experienced many hardships that only dedicated parents of a disabled child would know. During the early part of our ministry in that church, Kay was hired part-time as a teacher's aide in the special education department of a local school. Would you believe she was assigned to care for Laurie Tolker[7]?! Talk about God's beautiful plan unfolding. For two years Kay accompanied her during school bus rides and cared for her during class. My dear wife found tremendously deep healing for her own soul as she related with Laurie who carried the very same physical struggles that our Jeanie would have had. A bond formed. We thanked God many times for bringing us through this new cycle of healing. It was "beyond anything we could have asked or imagined." (Ephesians 3:20) For us, it was a tangible demonstration of Jesus' words "I have told you these things, so that in me you may have peace. In this world you will have trouble. But take heart! I have overcome the world." (John 16:33 NIV)

For us, those words came to mean "joy in the midst of grief!" Joy was a very special word for Kay. Today it can be found in one place or another in many locations in our home.

I have already told you that a rock solid faith in God will not necessarily shield you from difficulty.

In fact, that's a promise. Jesus said in Matthew 6:34, "Today's trouble is enough for today." Again in John 16:33 he said, "In this world, you have trouble." (NIV) Did someone in your life tell you that if you would trust Jesus, you would have no more stress? Jesus himself does not say that. Many people are understandably attracted to the thought that the Messiah should bring better times. In fact, many Old Testament passages hold out the hope that the coming Christ will set things right for the nation of Israel. Today, we can look at Jesus' own claims and realize that his kingdom is not of this world, as he said in John 18:36. Yet, are we really *no* better off in this life for believing Christ? This is a question worth considering as we evaluate the Old Testament in light of what Jesus said about it.

In the Gospel of Mark, the stage was set for understanding the theme of joy in the midst of heartache, in that the Priests and Pharisees rejected the "70 x 7 love" of God in Jesus Christ. "The Stone the Builders rejected has become the head of the corner." (Mark 12:10). They rejected the only love which could do what was done for Kay and for the Tolker family. THIS is the kind of love God offers through Jesus: "Then Peter came to Jesus and asked, "Lord, how often should I forgive someone who sins against me? Seven times?" "No, not seven times,"

Jesus replied, *"but seventy times seven!"* Matthew 18:21-22 (NLT) Some Bible translations use the phrase "seventy-seven times" instead, but Jesus certainly did not intend seventy-seven to be a limit on God's grace, so I prefer the "seventy times seven". God's "70 x 7 love" is powerful and releases us from the burden of thinking that our sin caused Jeanie's death, which some verses in the Old Testament seem to teach. There are many verses in Deuteronomy that tell us bad things happen because God is punishing us for our sins.

Let's say your child has died or you have fallen sick or lost your home. You will find in Deuteronomy that these events are your own fault for having disobeyed one of God's commandments. The entire book of Deuteronomy puts forth the "blessings and curses" rules. These are if/then statements, such as 28:1-2: "If you will only obey the Lord your God, by diligently observing all his commandments that I am commanding you today, the Lord your God will set you high above all the nations of the earth; all these blessings shall come upon you and overtake you, if you obey the Lord your God." (Deuteronomy 28:1-2) The passage goes on to list some of the blessings including fertility in childbearing, success in farming and finances, defeat and banishment of your enemies, and having others be afraid of you. Although "diligently observing all his commandments" differs from simply believing in God, it is not hard to see why so many people have believed the mistaken idea that trust in God will keep away all our earthly struggles.

However, the same chapter in Deuteronomy goes on to show a disturbing alternative. Verse 15 says, "But if you will not obey the Lord your God by diligently observing all his commandments and decrees, which I am commanding you today, then all these curses shall come upon you and overtake you." To be cursed by God would mean infertility, ruined crops, sick animals, confusion, and sickness including wasting diseases. You will be defeated militarily and then be struck with such things as boils and blindness.

Does any of this sound like the God of Jesus Christ? The One described in John 3:16-17? "For God so loved the world that he gave his only Son, so that everyone who believes in him may not perish but may have eternal life. Indeed, God did not send the Son into the world to condemn the world, but in order that the world might be saved through him."? No!

Note that Deuteronomy also promises in 4:40 that these rules will be in place *"for all time."* If we accept the idea that the old covenant is perfect and perfectly recorded and applicable forever, we would have to conclude that the death of my baby daughter at two hours old was God's curse on me or my wife for disobeying one or more of God's commandments at some point in our lives.

But Jesus challenges the system of blessings and curses described in Deuteronomy. The Sermon on the Mount in Matthew chapters 5, 6, and 7 is a good place to start looking at what Jesus' teaches about them. In these chapters we have a compilation of the main themes of Jesus' teachings.

A very clear refutation is found in Jesus' words in Matthew 5:45: "…for he makes his sun rise on the evil and on the good and sends rain on the righteous and on the unrighteous." This doesn't sound at all like the verses in Deuteronomy which tell us that curses are the result of a person's sins. For those of us who have endured tragedies such as the death of a child or spouse, or the loss of a home, or have been stricken with disease, it is good news indeed that these were not caused by our sins of the past. The Good News is that God's love goes with us through the hardships, and we can find healing and joy in the midst of the trouble. Again, we truly find comfort in Jesus' words which are John 16:33. "I have told you these things, so that in me you may have peace. In this world you will have trouble. But take heart! I have overcome the world." (NIV)

Jesus offers several other challenges to the Old Testament laws, which we can recognize by Jesus' words, "You have heard it said (followed by an Old Testament Law) … but I say to you…". (Matthew chapter 5:21, 27, 31, 33, 38, 43). Let's look at one of these sayings in detail.

"You have heard that it was said, 'You shall love your neighbor and hate your enemy', But I say to you, Love your enemies and pray for those who persecute you so that you may be sons of your Father who is in heaven. For he makes his sun rise on the evil and on the good, and sends rain on the just and on the unjust." Matthew 5:43-45

If try to find "you shall love your neighbor and hate your enemy" in the Old Testament using a concordance or simply a search tool, you will not find those precise words together. In this Matthew passage, Jesus gives a summary of Old Testament teaching here rather than a word for word quote. To those who study the Old Testament thoroughly, the admonition to hate enemies is not surprising at all. The point is that Jesus actually changes our instructions. He not only turned Old Testament teaching on its head, but he went so far as to equate loving one's enemy with becoming a child of God.

In light of the Old Testament teachings, especially in Leviticus, Numbers, and Deuteronomy, the way to be considered blessed by God is threefold. First, be born into (or possibly marry into[8]) one of the twelve tribes of Israel. Second, you must avoid all sin. And third, you must keep every ceremonial law listed in the five books of the Old Testament (often called "Torah" or "Pentateuch".) In the words of The Complete Jewish Bible[9], the Messiah did indeed "explain the obscure passages of Torah and actually change it." Jesus leaves us little room to argue this point if we take Matthew 5 seriously.

But what about Jesus' own words in Matthew 5:17-20? "Do not think that I have come to abolish the law or the prophets; I have come not to abolish, but to fulfill. For truly I tell you, until heaven and earth pass away, not one letter, not one stroke of a letter, will pass away until all is accomplished. Therefore, whoever breaks one of the least of these commandments, and teaches others to do the same, will be called least in the kingdom of heaven, but whoever does them and teaches them will be called great in the Kingdom of Heaven. For I tell you, unless your righteousness exceeds that of the scribes and Pharisees, you will never enter the Kingdom of Heaven." Matthew 5:17-20

Which is it? Did he come to change the Law as discussed in the previous paragraph, or did he come to fulfill the Law as these verses state? This a fair question, and it has an answer, though it may not be the anticipated one. I have pondered for years the meaning of the four verses in Matthew 5:17-20. They seem to speak of Jesus coming to fulfill the Law and the Prophets, as follows:

At first glance, the above verses appear to disagree with the thrust of Hebrews 8:6-7 that we considered in Chapter 1. Yet remember that before chapter five of Matthew is finished, Jesus repeats six times: "You have heard that it was said to those of old . . . but I say to you . . ." You can see that Jesus is offering real contrast.

As the Messiah, Jesus is the Living Word of God made flesh and has the authority to make these changes in Law. However, during his ministry on earth, Jesus said he had come to complete "The Law and The Prophets." As we have already seen, the New Law of Jesus is superior to the old covenant, and the old covenant needed completing because it was imperfect. Christ is thus the "canon" or "rule" that determines what is Christ-like in the writings we know as the Bible. This is huge and must not be passed over.

Let's take it a little further. Matthew 5:46-48 contains the very essence of Jesus' understanding of the nature of God:

"For if you love those who love you, what reward do you have? Do not even the tax collectors do the same? And if you greet only your brothers and sisters, what are you doing more than others? Do not even the Gentiles do the same? Be perfect, therefore, as your heavenly Father is perfect." ("Perfect" can easily be translated "all-merciful.")

What is going on here? These powerful words speak of great contrast with instructions in the Old Testament, yet many treatments of Jesus' words about fulfilling the Covenant seem to be at odds with Hebrews 8:6-7. Thoughts range from seeing the New Testament as a carbon copy of the Old, to saying the New Testament fulfills the spirit of the law but not always the "letter" of the Law.

However, in Deuteronomy 11:1 Moses clearly says that all of the decrees, commandments and ordinances are to be kept forever. Yet how many Christians actually feel bound to them? The Sabbath laws alone, if they were to be required of us today, carry the death penalty for serious failures to observe. I have described details from just one small section, but there are many more in the Torah. How can people want to advocate the veracity of the entire Old Testament, while just sweeping such facts under the rug?

Again:

"But Jesus has now obtained a more excellent ministry, and to that degree he is the mediator of a better covenant, which has been enacted through better promises. For if that first covenant had been faultless, there would have been no need to look for a second one." Hebrews 8:6-7

Why is it that these two verses seem to have so little weight among some Christian believers? I find there is something close to a conspiracy of silence among people who want to believe that all of the Bible is of one piece. They seem to fear that faith in the Bible cannot stand examination. They are dodging the issue that at certain points, the Bible itself (in its Old Testament portion) is the source of disagreement with Jesus' teachings about enemies. For those unfamiliar with the particulars, it may be helpful to know that what we call the Old Testament was at the time of Jesus a collection of scrolls in two main categories: The Law, which is found in the first five books: Genesis, Exodus, Leviticus, Numbers, and Deuteronomy, and The Prophets, which were also considered sacred and consist of Isaiah, Jeremiah, Ezekiel, and the last twelve books in the Old Testament. There is a third section of the Old Testament called The Writings: Esther, Job, Psalms, Proverbs, Ecclesiastes, the Song of Solomon, Ruth, Lamentations, Daniel, and Ezra. The Writings were not considered to be part of the fully inspired Word of God at that time, but they were considered important and Jesus was aware of them.

Some Bible Scholars in dealing with "fulfilling" the Law do not go on to "fulfilling the prophets", this latter being an integral part of Jesus' position statement. Fulfilling the Prophets ought to have something to do with their critiques of the Old Testament covenant concerning the use of animal slaughter in the sacrificial system of the Temple. Micah 6:6-8 bravely challenged the Pentateuch's assumptions in relating the animal sacrifices to the atonement for sin. When one speaks concerning such things, they are dealing with a very large part of the Old Testament.

In that light, how powerful the words of Micah are:

"With what shall I come before the Lord, and bow myself before God on high? Shall I come before him with burnt offerings, with calves a year old? Will the Lord be pleased with thousands of rams, with ten thousands of rivers of oil? Shall I give my first born for my transgression, the fruit of my body for the sin of my soul?

"He has told you, O mortal, what is good; and what does the Lord require of you but to do justice, and to love kindness, and to walk humbly with your God?" Micah 6:6-8

The Letter to the Hebrews throughout its pages exposes the inefficacy of removing guilt through the sacrifice of animals as clearly taught in large parts of the Old Testament. God's love in Christ "made perfect by sacrifice" (Hebrews 2:10, 4:8, 10:20) is the answer to Micah's question. Though there is a tendency for commentators to say that Jesus did not actually come out against animal sacrifice, their supposition is not true.

But there is a principle of interpretation Jesus used in Matthew 19:3 when he was approached by some Pharisees with the question: "Is it lawful for a man to divorce his wife for any cause?" They were lifting up Moses' laws against what Jesus said in in the Sermon on the Mount about divorce, (Matthew 5:31-32) namely that no divorce will be given. Whatever you think about that, Jesus knew that women were not allowed that same option as men to enact divorce, and to Jesus this was a sin against

God's plan in creation. Follow Jesus' answer carefully:

"He answered, 'Have you not read that the one who made them at the beginning 'made them male and female?''" Matthew 19:4 (Jesus quoting Genesis 1:27)

"For this reason a man shall leave his father and mother and be joined to his wife, and the two shall become one flesh." Matthew 19:5 (Jesus quoting Genesis 2:24)

The Pharisees parried with the question: "Why then did Moses command us to give a certificate of dismissal and to divorce her?" (Matthew 19:7) Jesus' answer makes it clear that Moses compromised due to the hardness of men's hearts but "From the beginning it was not so." (Matthew 19:8) We might note that in another place (Mark 3:28) Jesus announced that all manner of sins would be forgiven except for blasphemy against the Holy Spirit. Divorce is not an unforgivable sin.

The reason that blasphemy against the Holy Spirit cannot be forgiven is that the Holy Spirit is the active agency in forgiveness. Many people miss the fact that some blasphemies will be forgiven, which strengthens the point. The solution is to humbly re-open oneself to the Holy Spirit of grace, both in this life and the life to come.

The word of Jesus to the Pharisees implies that "from the beginning" it was not God's purpose to subjugate women to men but to be as one, or "one flesh." Jesus' entire New Covenant provides a way of getting back to God's intentions in creation.

The Gospel of John has a very high sense of the Divinity of Jesus, surpassing that of the other Gospels. As John put it in chapter 1:18 the Living Word of Creation was fully in Jesus Christ. It is out of that "imprint of the Divine" that Jesus could reflect on his own past with the Creator God whom he addressed as Father. (John 17:5) But in John 1:12-13 we read:

"But to all who received him, who believed in his name, he gave power to become children of God, who were born, not of blood or of the will of the flesh or of the will of man, but of God."

This language of a birth not of blood, or the will of flesh, or the will of man, is the same logic applied to Jesus as the "only Begotten" Son of God in John 3:16. In truth, the early church father Athanasius said, "Jesus became human that we might become divine." The principle of John that holds these two facts about Jesus in creative tension is apparent in his words to Nicodemus in John 3:6, "What is born of the flesh is flesh, and what is born of the spirit is spirit."

I have heard critics of the Gospel say, "I would be willing to follow Jesus if I thought I too could be a son or daughter of God." Well, Paul proclaimed in Galatians 3:26, "In Christ Jesus you are all Children of God through faith." As creatures of God we are loved of God, but through faith in Jesus Christ, and the New Kingdom of Heaven Law of Love, we *are* daughters and sons of God.

The Old and New Testaments are best understood in the teaching and healing ministry of Jesus. My father, the late Rev. James O McClarey, grew up in the so-called Bible Belt of Tennessee. As a child, I often heard Dad speak with greater than usual force when quoting the words of Jesus: "You have heard that it was said to those of old…. *but I say to you.*" His voice would boom, and his eyes would glisten when he got to that part of the sermon. I did years of study to understand the rational reasons behind the force of my father's fierce devotion. Dad intuitively sensed that something greater had come in Jesus.

JUDGING THE HEALING POWER OF JESUS

Indeed, something greater did arrive on earth when Jesus began his ministry, just as he announced in the synagogue in Nazareth: "Today this scripture has been fulfilled in your hearing." (Luke 4:21) One of the most impressive aspects of the ministry of Jesus was the healings he performed; yet these miracles are also a stumbling block for the faith of many people today. Very early on, Matthew reports that Jesus traveled all over Galilee, teaching and performing many healings, to the extent that Jesus became famous for all kinds of healings and was much sought after for them. (Matthew 4:23-24)

Some people have trouble believing that the healings happened in the first place, and some cannot believe that healings are possible today. If you do not relate to one of these, perhaps you are a person who can accept healing miracles in general, but you have a hard time believing that healing could be available to you. We will touch on all of these. One of my old friend Mort's conundrums was "if God never changes, why doesn't God do healing miracles any more?" This is one of those "unsafe questions" in some Christian circles and therefore one of the reasons I wrote this book. It is okay to ask your questions and to have them considered seriously. After all, how many healing miracles have we seen in our lifetimes?

All four Gospels emphasize the numerous healings performed by Jesus (and later by his disciples). They can be looked at in more than one category, however. Jesus healings were more than "Zap! You are Healed!" He conversed with people, sometimes answering a spiritual need as part of a physical remedy and at times even indicating that a person was actually healed by his or her own faith. He often tied in the need for forgiveness and wholeness with his concept of wellness. Jesus combined real and recognized medicines along with his knowledge of what would work for a given person. This may have included the use of standard medicines available at the time, such as wine as a guard against infection or oil as a soothing lubricant.

One possible example of Jesus healing through superior medical understanding is the daughter of Jairus described in both Mark 5 and Luke 8. Jesus was told that the girl was dead, but he told the crowd that this child was not dead, but sleeping. The group laughed at him, for as far as they could see, she was dead. Jesus took her by the hand and said, "Little girl, I say to you, arise." The girl rose up, and Jesus told the parents to give her something to eat. People coming out of a coma often need something to eat. Jesus' counter-diagnosis was apparently correct.

This is not to say that Jesus never raised anyone from the dead. Of course, we know that he did.[10] Talking about Jesus using tools of medicine or psychology does not take anything away from his spiritual power to perform miracles. Rather, it brings modern medicine and psychology into the realm of God's work today. Jesus, as the Messiah and as the Word of God, had access to knowledge in many areas of expertise, some that were understood at the time and some that were ahead of his time.

Another example of Jesus using little known therapies is in Mark 8:22 near the town of Bethsaida. A blind man is brought to Jesus who puts saliva on the man's eyes, touches him and then asks, "Can you see anything?" The man looks up and says, "I see people, but they look like trees, walking." Then Jesus lays his hands on the man's eyes a second time, and then "he saw everything clearly." This miracle has an interesting geographical component. Note that Jesus "led him out of the village" (8:23) and then later told him not to return to the village. (8:26) Though we are not explicitly told why, perhaps it had something to do with Jesus' rebuke of Bethsaida for not repenting. (Matthew 11:21-24)

In Luke 8, we have a miracle taking place in a geographical setting that seems important in a different way. A man who had lived naked in tombs and in chains approaches Jesus, kneels down and screams: "'What have you to do with me, Jesus, Son of the most high God? I beg you do not torment me.' Jesus asked him, 'What is your name?'" (8:28) There is a type of relational logic which holds that if we can name our fears, we can control them. The man answered, "My name is Legion, for we are many." (8:30) Psychiatrists in our time might well call this a case of multiple personality, which is very hard to cure. It could also have been a case of the "Military Battle Syndrome." Apparently, Jesus came to a similar conclusion. When people saw what was going on, they ran to bring some people to observe. When they arrived, the man was sitting at the feet of Jesus, implying that he was listening and learning, and he was "fully clothed and in his right mind." (8:35)

This man wanted to follow Jesus, but the Lord told him to go back to his own townspeople and tell them the good news. Why do you think Jesus recommended this instead of taking the man with him? It is quite possible that the townspeople who knew the man would be more apt to be aware of the changes in him. It is no accident that Luke, "The Good Physician," was the one who gave us this insight.

Think of today's touch therapies, holistic medicine practices, and much in the field of psychology as modern examples of some of the skills that Jesus used along with his spiritual power. But even what we call "miracles of modern medicine" can be attributed to God's inspirations to scientists and medical practitioners. Have you ever prayed for God to provide a healing miracle through a surgery? There is nothing wrong with that, for it is because of the discoveries of God's truth that we have the knowledge to do surgeries.

Jesus was able like a good doctor to give prescriptions that brought the bodies and souls of people to wholeness. Certainly, the forgiving grace of God in Jesus Christ is a major part of becoming whole. Look in Luke 5 at the paralyzed man who was carried to Jesus by his friends. In a moment when we are expecting to see the man get up and walk, Jesus instead says, "Man, your sins are forgiven you." (5:20) The man later ends up walking home carrying his cot, but we see here that Jesus considered his spiritual release from bondage more important (and more difficult) than his release from the physical bondage of paralysis.

In John 9, we see a healing miracle that is not tied to forgiveness. A man born blind was seen by Jesus and his disciples. His disciples asked Jesus: "Rabbi, who sinned, this man or his parents, that he was born blind?" As we saw in chapter 2, the disciples had been taught to believe that disease was a punishment for sin, but they were not sure whether it was a person's own sin or that of his parents that might have caused the blindness. Jesus answered, "Neither." This had to come as a shock; no beating around the bush here. But in John 9:3 Jesus takes the positive approach in saying that this was an opportunity to do a helpful thing. In this case, the man received his sight when Jesus simply spoke saying, "receive your sight."

John 5 has an interesting mix of spiritual and physical healing. "One man had been an invalid for thirty-eight years. When Jesus saw him lying there and knew that he had already been there a long time, he said to him, 'Do you want to be healed?'" (5:5-6) This reminds me of a movie from the 1940s called The Prince of Peace. I recall a little girl coming to Jesus, asking him to fix her broken doll. Jesus reached out to work on it, but she hugged it tightly. Then as she gazed at his loving smile, she released it to him in childlike trust, and he repaired the doll. That was masterful because that's the way we are with are with God at times. There are times, it seems, when our willingness to trust God is important in the healing.

Not always though. There were and are people who were healed because of the prayers of others. The twelve year old daughter of Jairus would likely have died in her coma if not for the request her father made to Jesus. (Luke 8) Also the Syro-Phoenician woman who asked for healing for her daughter was granted that request. (Matthew 15) The Roman Centurion who Jesus remarked had greater faith than he had seen elsewhere was asking not for his own healing but that of a servant of his household. (Matthew 8)

A lot comes out about Jesus' personality and mission in studying his healings. The woman who had a twelve year condition of hemorrhaging touched the fringe of Jesus' garment. Jesus, with the crowd around Him, asks, "Who touched me?" He sensed that "power" had gone out of him." (Luke 8:45-46) Passages like this speak to us of the human side of Jesus as well as the divine side.

Sometimes God sends help through people. Over the years of our ministry, Kay and I had many friends, and none dearer friends than Don and Elsie

Westerman. Not once or just twice, but three times, we entrusted them with the care of our two children during times of crisis. Don and Elsie were the friends who got the midnight call from me the night of our losing Jeanie. Our daughter and son, ages 7 and 5, knew them well enough to leave with Don who came to the hospital emergency room while I stayed near Kay and the new baby. That visit was much longer than anticipated. A short time later, when Kay's father died in a tragic accident, Don and Elsie again came through to care for Jan and Jimmy. And later when I broke several bones in a church softball game, who do you think was caring for our children while Kay attended me at the hospital? Elsie and Don again. Sometimes healing comes as joy in the midst of grief. Sometimes it comes as friends in times of trouble.

More recently, a friend in our community was healed of painful shingles in a quiet worship and prayer service attended by only about twenty people. Betty's spirit was lifted mightily as a result, and we were all frankly amazed to see God tending to her physical pain in this modern day miracle of healing.

Then and now, healing can be physical, mental, spiritual, or relational. We may find it harder to believe the physical healings, but the spiritual healings are no less impressive. Certainly, one of the most important healings in my own life has to do with my and my wife's emotional healing following the death of our infant daughter so many years ago. At last, I can tell you the rest of that story.

You may remember that we knew Laurie Tolker[11], the girl who was born on the same day our Jeanie was. One of the Tolkers' concerns during Laurie's growing up was that, at thirteen, she had not been able to attend confirmation classes for church membership. Kay brought this to my attention. There were several practical barriers to her being able to attend the class with the other children, so I offered to hold a private confirmation class.

After she completed the classes, when the time came for her to be confirmed in the church, Laurie told me she wanted to sing a song during the service. This surprised me, not being aware that she could sing. But I gave her the go-ahead.

That Sunday morning, at the moment chosen for her, she rolled forward in her wheelchair, waited for the music, and sang with a singularly beautiful voice.

The lyrics of the song went something like this. "I asked the Lord of creation if, in all this universe, there is a place and a time that are mine. And God said to me that, yes, there is a place, and a time, that are mine."

I was able to look through my tears enough to see that there wasn't a dry eye in the place. Now I could only marvel at the blessing of Laurie's life. This was a true completion of the healing I experienced.

4

JUDGING THE HUMAN ASPECT OF JESUS

For centuries people have debated the balance between intellect and experience in matters of faith. When some people feel that intellect is overly emphasized, there are people who react with statements such as, "You can't think your way into heaven!" When experience is overly emphasized, others may respond with a reminder that God created us with brains and intended for us to use them.

My father was not educated beyond the eighth grade, but as mentioned at the end of Chapter 2 he had an intuitive spiritual sense that Jesus was uniquely from God and that Jesus transcended the Old Testament. Dad was intelligent though not formally educated. Unfortunately there were people in his life that held his lack of formal education against him. Jesus however, did not seem to make judgments on such things. He seemed to be comfortable with people wherever they were, and he showed that he could match wits with lawyers and scribes.

As is usually the case, Jesus offers a position which is not "either/or" but rather "both/and.". He related with people who were educated and uneducated, people who tried to trap him intellectually and people whose sanity was in question. (See Luke 8:26-39.) Jesus would be comfortable with my father and his informal education, with Laurie Tolker whose oxygen deprivation at birth left her with a less than fully developed mental capacity, with my friend Mort and his deep questions about faith.

There have been criticisms of Jesus in recent years regarding whether or not he was in fact educated. I believe he was, and I will lay out my argument by exploring the question, "Did Jesus have scribes?" This is an important question because people who have severe questions about faith, such as Mort, need to see that the object of our faith stands up to rigorous intellectual scrutiny.

Did Jesus Have Scribes?

Of course not, you may be saying. After all, you may have heard quite the opposite; that is, Jesus was unlettered and given to simple stories. Along with this you've probably been told that the common people heard Jesus gladly and always understood him; perhaps you have been informed that the first writings about Jesus took place after the disciples saw the need to leave records only after years of verbal propagation of the Gospel.

There are extremely strong indications that the New Testament had behind it written sources much earlier than is usually maintained. This is important to consider as we ask the question: Did Jesus have scribes? But you may be asking, "What difference does it make?" More than ever before, the importance of Jesus Christ in issues of life is being subjected to a certain "minimization." Just as we minimize a document on our computers to push it aside temporarily and then forget it is still there, some of us are minimizing Jesus while we go on with our lives as if we have forgotten Christ. Some of the scariest trends are right under our noses. Minimization of Jesus can come from all directions, whether left, right, center or similar categories of thought and practice. Consequently, something needs to be done to curtail the deterioration of Christian faith that comes with making Jesus less than he was.

One of the minimizing trends has to do with peeling away at the New Testament characterization of Jesus as having outstanding wisdom. With that wisdom he not only impressed those who were described as "common" but also the intelligentsia. Had Jesus been as illiterate as some have claimed, the leading thinkers of Israel would not have bothered to debate with him.

This circumventing of the profile of Jesus is having repercussions in our time; no doubt in our day the pulling away from the faith of many people who have serious doubts about the Bible is in part rooted in the downward manipulation of the character of Jesus. People who have doubts do not all belong to one strata of society and they need to be heard. Many churches have within their membership or former membership people who feel that they are not being helped with their questions. Instead of scolding them, we need to offer strong thinking and informed compassion.

Another level of concern, as shown in Chapter 1, is that if Jesus is not who he was lifted up to be in the New Testament, how can His views and actions have any power over the unspeakably cruel concepts of the Lord in the Old Testament? Answers may be sitting in ivory towers as scholastic files, but they have not been greatly forthcoming.

It is obvious from the records that the same people who heard Jesus gladly were astounded with his wisdom, and thought it beyond what they were used to hearing. Furthermore, they did not always understand him, at least at first; Jesus often asked, "Don't you yet understand?" Whether Jesus had scribes is intimately bound together with the manner in which his piercing insights caused all kinds of people to take notice. Even more, it is quite possible that the earliest writings after Jesus' death were provided by such scribes.

There are scholars who maintain that Jesus could not read. When you take the approach of invalidating something, you have to change other things in order to make the disclaimers consistent. If you want to say that Jesus could not read, you have to ignore the entire fourth chapter of Luke, which reports Jesus reading from scripture at his home town in Nazareth. You would also have to treat as spurious the three recorded instances of Jesus asking people, "Haven't you read?" Why would he ask such a question if he was not himself a reader?

It was not only Jesus' predictions of his death that upset the Disciples; they just didn't get it when Jesus knelt to wash the feet of the disciples before the crucifixion. Had they understood their own scriptures, as Jesus did, their outlook would have been markedly different. Jesus spoke in a parabolic and metaphoric manner, which sometimes met with humorous reactions, as when they brought him bread to eat when he was talking about other than earthly bread. This caused Jesus to say, "I have bread to eat that you don't know about."John 4:31-34

As an example of slowness to understand the ways of Jesus, in John 13 Jesus washes the feet of the Disciples but faces an emotional display when it came to Peter's turn. Jesus said to him, "You do not know now what I am doing, but later you will understand." (John 13:7) This not only lifts up the importance of understanding but also Jesus' deep knowledge of the nature of human beings. Is it a stretch to think that Jesus would also have used scribes to record the stories and sayings he knew would not be fully comprehended until after his death and resurrection?

Indications of Early Writings about Jesus

There are several data that can be traced in the New Testament which indicate that writings about Jesus did exist before 50 AD. The Apostle Paul in I Corinthians 15:3, says to a group of early church leaders, "I handed on to you as of first importance what I in turn had received: that Christ died for our sins in accordance with the scriptures, and that he was buried, and that he was raised on the third day in accordance with the scriptures…" The word "handed" implies something material, not just oral reports. In the NRSV-NIV Parallel New Testament in Greek and English,[12] the Greek word *paredoka* is used, and translated "For I delivered…" which has the same connotation.

This action of Paul was a <u>past</u> event. Paul's earliest Corinthian letters have, along with the Q corpus, been said to be among the first actual writings associated with the propagation of the Good News.

The context seems to indicate that the items handed to Paul had only to do with the passion and resurrection of Jesus. There is a passage in Philippians 2:6-11 that speaks of Jesus Christ in his divine side coming into the world to be a servant that is often said to be a composed hymn. The hymn, if not written by Paul on the occasion of writing his letter, would have pre-dated the letter; indeed, that is the contention of many who speak this way. So, along with the basic written story of the passion and resurrection, we have a hymn in writing.

The New Testament does make reference at times to teachings of Jesus outside the Gospels. Paul in I Thessalonians 4:11[13] called on the Christians of Thessalonica to "work with their own hands." This refers back to I Thessalonians 4:2 which lifts up the "instructions we gave you through the Lord Jesus Christ." Later, in II Thessalonians 3:12 he appeals "in the Lord Jesus Christ" for everyone to work with their own hands instead of depending on the church for income. This implies a teaching of Jesus. The notion that Paul knew nothing of Jesus' teachings, and taught only a religion of salvation through the cross, is thus seriously questioned.

Sometimes The Apostle Paul would say, as he sought to deal with problems of churches he had founded, "I have no word of the Lord on this." The flip side is that the many pronouncements Paul made were traceable, verbally or in written form, to Jesus.

In Acts 20:35 Paul mentions Jesus' teaching, "It is more blessed to give than to receive." Does this not call to mind the words of Jesus, "Give, expecting nothing in return"? Paul in Romans 12:17 said to the members of the church in Rome, "Repay no one evil for evil," the exact essence of Jesus' words in Matthew 5:38-39 about avoiding retaliation against evildoers. These examples provide also an argument against the contention that the New Testament is filled with disagreement. These attributions, though small in number, indicate that Paul had a gift for boiling down a larger group of teachings into a few words.

There is no strong reason that some of Jesus' teachings as well as written indications of his suffering, death and resurrection could not have come to Paul in written form very soon after his conversion. Consequently it is not necessary to ascribe a date as late as 50 AD for the first Q writings. After all, if Q, as a written document, had to do with the pristine, original Jesus, was the oral period of the Gospel "Pre Pristine?" or perhaps "Pre original?" Absurd!

There has been little made of the fifteen days that Paul spent with the Apostle Peter, as mentioned in Galatians 1:18. Since Peter, according to a sound tradition involving an early church leader named Papias,[14] shared with the disciple Mark information that became the Gospel of Mark, would that not have been an opportunity for him to convey to Paul a great deal about the life, death, teachings, actions and resurrection of Jesus?

Scribes in the Old Testament

Any worthwhile study of scribes within the pages of the Bible must include the Old Testament. Since we are dealing with a significant breakthrough that challenges views held for centuries, we must cover the important bases. For starters, it is well known that the Prophet Jeremiah had a scribe named Baruch, (Jeremiah 36:26), who is repeatedly mentioned in chapters 32-46. Baruch recorded a religious vision of Jeremiah. In addition to this, he had charge of legal documents such as deeds of purchase (Jeremiah 32:1-15), and he probably had a special chamber in the Royal Palace. (Jeremiah 36:10).

In I Chronicles 24:6, we observe that a scribe named Shemaiah recorded the details of the re-organization of the priesthood at the time of King David. Later, in I Chronicles 27:36 we read that Jonathan, King David's uncle, was a counselor, being a man of understanding and a scribe. This shows that scribes did far more than take notes. In II Kings 22:3ff, during the reign of highly regarded King Josiah, Shaphan the Scribe appears to be a minister of finance. In Isaiah 36:3, during the reign of Hezekiah, Shebna the Scribe was a kind of secretary of state. During the time of the rebuilding of the temple after the return from the Exile to Babylon, Ezra was identified as a "Scribe skilled in the Law of Moses." (Ezra 7:6)

At the time of Ezra and Nehemiah, when the people began to return from their captivity in Babylon, scribes played an important role as the walls of Jerusalem were repaired and the Temple was being rebuilt. During these years they emerged as a distinctive and influential professional class of teachers and interpreters of the Law. The scribes began to work with the priests, copying sacred scriptures, guarding them, and taking part in deciding what was to be considered sacred Scripture and what was not. This is the function generally known as "canonization".[15]

Scribes in the New Testament

Turning now to the New Testament era, according to the Interpreter's Dictionary of the Bible, there were "Scribes of the masses outside Jerusalem."[16] Luke 5:17 speaks of "Scribes drawn from every village in Galilee and Judea and from Jerusalem." The text reads at this point: "Pharisees and teachers of the law." The teachers of the law may well have been scribes.

Just about everybody had scribes! They were in the Sanhedrin. The Sadducees had them. The Essenes had them. The Elders had them and the Priests had them. They were often useful in providing documentation in times of upheaval and unrest.

The Phantom Scholars of John Dominic Crossan

It is quite interesting that John Dominic Crossan, a leader in the Jesus Seminar fellowship, seeks to fill in a significant portion of the supposed void of writing before 50 AD by conjecturing that very soon after Jesus' death on the cross, an educated group of Jesus' former followers sought to make sense of his death by "searching the scriptures."[17] Crossan believes that these "scribe types," were trying to make sense of Jesus' death in a way that would keep hope alive for their people. Though he and Dr. Borg have worked together, their position at this point seems to be at loggerheads. Crossan even seems to be inconsistent with his own thesis. This is no small matter; if no writing existed until twenty years after Jesus' death, and the followers of Jesus were, like him, poor, uneducated beggars, how can he speak of scribal types who have followed Jesus' career seriously enough that they seek to make sense of his death by searching the scriptures? Such "educated" types would either be scribes or have scribes. Why wouldn't *they* have produced some notes before 50 AD?

In another chapter Crossan contends that Jesus was a poor, illiterate peasant and mendicant who was surrounded by disciples in the same circumstances. He bases this on a social studies theory known as cross-cultural anthropology. According to Crossan's' use of that discipline, certain societies have an upper class and a lower class and no middle class.[18] That being so, it is quite a stretch to come out with a group of scholarly types who, immediately after losing their leader, begin theologizing about the cross.

If this is true, it opens the door to a class of people following Jesus rather closely who had scribal standing and dedicated their skills to accurate recording, or at the very least to an organized approach to memory. It also opens the door to those capabilities being in use during Jesus' earthly ministry, that is, by Jesus himself.

What I have found in examining the evidence has brought me to the conclusion that it would be surprising if Jesus *didn't* have scribes. He constantly pushed people beyond their usual biases and used a variety of means to open for them his great vision of a realm over which a smiling, hurting, loving, forgiving, inclusive and empowering God leads people through life's challenges to a joyful and triumphant end.

It is understandable that a vision so great would cause a deep inward churning of heart, soul, mind and strength among people who sought to find security through drawing into themselves. People do not easily give up their beliefs until they discover that there is something higher and better.

There is another level to the words: "the common people heard him gladly." Some interpreters imply that Jesus hung out almost exclusively with the people who were rather poor and were looked down upon by those in power. Yet we say at the same time Jesus loved everyone. That should mean that he was able to communicate with everyone. The mere tracing of Jesus' activities shows that Jesus indeed appealed to all classes. The Pharisees are often pictured as hostile to him, yet they invited him to banquets, interviewed him often, and even warned him when they felt he was in danger. One scribe called him "Teacher," (Rabbi in some translations) which would be odd if Jesus appeared to be uneducated. (Matthew 8:9)

The scribes, by the way, often served under someone who had authority over them; the priests had scribes as did the Elders and the Pharisees. Some served under the temple establishment, and thus also under the Romans who kept their fingers on things. There were two types of scribes, oral and writing. The oral scribes had very good memories and could recite vast amounts of material. The writing scribes were trained in interpreting religious or secular documents. Both types were appreciated for their particular expertise. In some cases they may have kept records of proceedings.

There are other analyses concerning the extent of literacy and poverty in the world of the Bible that must be laid alongside that of Crossan's' Cross-Cultural Analysis. According to the Oxford Bible Atlas, the world in which the Old Testament personalities moved was a literate world. Kings communicated with each other and with their servants in writing; they recorded their acts and their conquests on written tablets of stone or clay or wax. The records of commerce, dealings in real estate of all kinds, private contracts, and judicial decisions were attested and preserved in writing."[19] Though this concerns the Old Testament, it sets up what follows: About the middle of the second millennium experiments were afoot in some of the cities of Canaan in the matter of forming an alphabet. The essential sounds of Semitic speech were easy to accommodate. "Thus a system of writing based on simple sounds could make EVERY MAN HIS OWN SCRIBE."[20] Notice the potential of wide-spread literacy!

The Redefinition of "Carpenter"

It has often been pointed out that in the Aramaic language the word for "carpenter" referenced a highly trained person, including skill in using wood, metal and stone. Geza Vermes says, "In Talmudic sayings the Aramaic noun denoting Carpenter or Craftsman stands for a scholar or learned man."[21] Joseph, the father of Jesus may well have been in such a company. Thus Galilee was not only filled with folks of the fishing industry, but also people strong in their faith and skilled in various crafts. It has also been mentioned that Joseph being described in Matthew as a "devout" man implied learning in the Talmud as well as strict adherence to its precepts.

Those who have seen the house belonging to the Apostle Peter in Capernaum, one of the more highly probable archaeological finds as to origin, have noticed that it contained quite a number of rooms. It is true that it may have housed an extended family, but it may also be that Peter was among the more successful fishermen in the company of Jesus. There are signs that early Christians may have met there, and the story in Matthew 8:5-17 is most fascinating in its intertwining of Jesus' healing of a Roman Centurion's Servant, and his later healing of Peter's mother-in-law at Peter's house.

Just a few paces from the home owned by Peter, there are the remains of a synagogue; while this synagogue has been dated to the fourth century, there is a foundation underneath made of black basalt, which is much older than the lighter colored stoned used in building on the foundation. There was a tradition that a Roman Centurion had built the Synagogue for the people of Capernaum. Is it possible that Jesus was dealing with that very Centurion as he healed the man's servant? Jesus' words about the centurion in the Matthew 8:5-17 story were to the effect that he had never seen greater faith in all of Israel than this man showed in trusting Jesus to effect this healing. This is but another incident revealing Jesus' ability to deal with all kinds of people.

But what of Jesus himself? While Jesus was still in Nazareth, he may well have worked alongside Joseph in the city of Sepphoris [22] and exposed to high levels of Greek and Roman Culture. Sepphoris was within walking distance from Nazareth. Jesus, it must be said, did not undertake his special calling from God until about age thirty. (Luke 2:23) This left him years to learn Joseph's trade as a worker in wood, metal and stone as an apprentice. Though Jesus' parents, while Jesus was a baby, paid the temple tax of a pair of turtledoves (Luke 2:24), denoting their poor estate at the time, chances are that as Joseph plied his trade, and Jesus after him, that the family could have been much more comfortable. It is highly possible that Jesus, who taught that his followers should give, expecting no return, devoted his earnings to the "common purse" used by the Apostles for their alms and their presentations of the Good News.

This array of historical notes offers at least a partial challenge to the claim of an absolute gap between the wealthy and the poor before and during the time of Jesus, especially in Galilee. This "gap-theory" also would have been largely untrue of the many non-Jews who preceded the resettled Jews. The Gentile leaders and tradespeople among the influx of skilled Jewish transplants likewise changed the nature of Galilee.

Probing the Mystery of an Overlooked Saying of Jesus

It is now time to zero in on a power-packed, but much neglected verse in the New Testament. In Matthew 13:51-52, there is a most interesting teaching of Jesus. After three brief parables on the Kingdom of Heaven, Jesus asked the disciples, "Have you understood all this?" They answered "Yes." And he said to them:

"Therefore every scribe trained in the Kingdom of heaven is like the master of a household who brings out of his treasure what is new and what is old."

One day while reading this it hit me! If Jesus said such a thing what became of it? Was it a plan he never had a chance to play out? As far as I know, very little has been done to follow up the apparent enigma. I did take up the matter quite seriously, and was not disappointed. Not only that, the findings are consistent with the profile of Jesus provided in the New Testament.

In the New Testament there are almost three times as many occurrences of the word "scribe" or its plural form (sixty three) as in the Hebrew Scriptures, (twenty three). Of course, one must allow for the fact that there are four Gospels, with the first three overlapping at many points. But there are a lot of Books of the Old Testament as well. This indicates a growing importance, particularly since the New Testament covers far fewer years than does the period for which we have the Hebrew Scriptures.

Let's consider some New Testament data: The word scribe or scribes appears 23 times in Matthew. Even more pertinent is the fact that in Matthew (8:18ff), a scribe came up to Jesus, saying "Rabbi, I will follow you wherever you go!"

Many people recognize that Jesus sometimes spoke of "Scribes and Pharisees" in a negative manner. Once he said, "Beware of the scribes, who like to walk around in long robes, and love to be greeted with respect in the marketplaces, and to have the best seats in the synagogues and places of honor at banquets. They devour widows' houses and for the sake of appearance say long prayers." (Luke 20:46-47) But this is just one side of the coin. We have only to compare Jesus' figure of speech of "leaven" as both a positive and negative symbol. On the positive side, it is used to portray the coming growth of the Kingdom of Heaven. (Mark 4:30-32) When Jesus spoke of the "Leaven of the Pharisees" in Matthew 16:6, that was negative.

So, there could be a positive orientation for the function of Scribe; in fact, those taught by Jesus would be open to old and new things that promoted the Kingdom of Heaven on earth, as over against holding on to the ways of the past. Many of the scribes, indeed, were aligned with leaders who wanted to cling to the past. Thus "Every Scribe trained in the Kingdom of Heaven shall be likened to a householder who takes out of his treasure things new and things old." (Matthew 13:52)

In Mark 12:28 a scribe, impressed with Jesus' response to a strong challenge from the Sadducees, that involved a profound analysis of an Old Testament scripture, came to Jesus and asked him "Which commandment is the first of all?" After Jesus gave his response, the Scribe was much moved, telling Jesus that he was absolutely right; not only that, but Jesus' understanding and vision were "much more important than all whole burnt offerings and sacrifices." Jesus response to him was significant: "You are not far from the Kingdom of God."

At the very moment I am writing this chapter, I am gazing at page 1881 of my Nelson's Complete Concordance on the Gospel references to Jesus as Teacher (or Rabbi). There are forty seven of them in a row. I am pleasantly shocked. Though the Gospels provide four versions of one story, they do have variety, and the usage of the title involves varying settings and a diverse population.

I am aware that long-held assumptions are not easy to let go, so I press on to additional data. The listing of scribes is important, but even more crucial is the specific manner in which the use of scribes evolved to their function at the time of Jesus. Remember that the Interpreter's Dictionary of the Bible explains [23] "The original scribe, or sopher, was a person able to "cipher" and from this came the meaning of "secretary" or "scribe". In the days before the Exile that began after the Destruction of Jerusalem in 586 BC, the Scribes took care of many "secular" functions even though they were part of a theocracy which combined the religious and the secular. However, when the government of Judah was being dismantled by the Babylonians, the Priests began to take over the functions that had belonged to the Scribes.

At the time of Ezra and Nehemiah, when the people began to return from their captivity in Babylon, Scribes played an important role as the walls of Jerusalem were repaired and the Temple was being rebuilt. During these years they emerged as a distinctive and influential professional class of teachers and interpreters of the Law. The Scribes began to work with the priests, copying sacred scriptures, guarding them, and taking part in deciding what was to be considered sacred Scripture and what was not. This is the function generally known as "canonization", which is the process by which decisions were made as to what writings could be considered part of the sacred scriptures. [24]

The Scribes were also the "wise men" of Proverbs, (not to be confused with the Wise Men of the story of Jesus' birth). Daniel 11:32-35 speaks of the wise men of the people, who are scribes. The Interpreter's Dictionary also comments that the scribes gathered Israel's sacred literature and interpreted it. In addition they were copyists, editors, and guardians of the textual purity of scripture. During the time of the Greek domination of Israel, which is reflected more in the Old Testament Apocryphal writings, the scribes became known as Pharisees and were lay people.[25]

Turning now to New Testament era, according to the Interpreter's Dictionary of the Bible, there were even "Scribes of the masses outside Jerusalem." (Matthew 7:29) And Luke 5:17 speaks of Scribes drawn from every village in Galilee and Judea and from Jerusalem! [26]

It is of special importance that in the Gospel of John, (John 8:3) there is only one mention of scribes; since it is generally held that John is the latest to be written of the four Gospels, this fact would undercut the often used argument that a particular practice reported to have taken place between Jesus and others had in fact to do with later conditions, and that the text in question was dubbed in later.

The contention of some scholars that the conflict of Jesus with the Pharisees had to do with a later time is a case in point. It is held that there were few Pharisees at the time of Jesus, and that they became more of a sore subject in the later church. Be that as it may, that argument would hold no force in the matter of scribes. In fact, it would point in the opposite direction. It points to the conditions surrounding the time of Jesus himself.

One of the most interesting cases in terms of our research has to do with Levi (Mark 2:14, Luke 5:27), the man Jesus recruited from the tax office. Levi became Matthew, the Apostle. The Gospel of Matthew alone has 23 references to scribes. Is this an accident? Luke has 14 references. Mark has 21 references; since his Gospel is usually said to be earlier than Matthew and Luke, plus the fact that Mark is a much shorter Gospel than Matthew or Luke, as well as being earlier....this has to be significant. The fact that Mark seems more interested in Jesus' eagerness and power in lifting up his Kingdom message, this is a matter of great significance.

What needs to emerge here is that according to a tradition of the Apostolic Fathers,[27] Papias, an early "church father" who learned from John the Elder, a follower of Jesus, that Simon Peter related to Mark his memoirs, who wrote them down as well as he could remember. In effect, Peter is using Mark as a scribe. Matthew/Levi was likely a scribe, as stated earlier; Luke, a long Gospel but one having a less direct pipeline to the original followers, naturally has fewer references to scribes. And John, probably the latest written of the Gospels, mentions only one. The weight of evidence has become considerable.

Even so, Luke, the "beloved physician", though not a disciple of Jesus during Jesus' physical life on earth, is often said to be the source of the "we" logs in the book of Acts which he authored. This is yet another example of writing and record keeping close to the time of Jesus, and that by a man, Luke, who as a doctor was probably well educated. Paul, whom Luke often accompanied, was writing up a storm in those days, as he founded churches. He had personal scribes mentioned by name; Sylvanus is mentioned in Thessalonians, (1:1 and 2:1) and more are mentioned in other letters of Paul. Only the "management" of the persona of Jesus that relegates him to the status of an uneducated beggar provides any cause to take him out of the arena of well-schooled persons, even among his closest followers. There is a reference to "uneducated" disciples (Acts 4:13) that some may use more widely than it was intended. Peter and John, who had been involved in healing and witness to Jesus, were the points of reference. This does not speak for all of the disciples. In fact there was probably a mix of backgrounds, which is consistent with Jesus' willingness to enter into fellowship with all kinds of people.

As to the literacy of Jesus, in spite of his words "Haven't you read?" (Matthew 12:3) being ruled out by some Jesus Seminar scholars due to "form criticism," Jesus is recorded in Matthew asking that question several times. (Matthew 12:3 & 5, 19:4, 21:16 & 42, and 22:31) This shows a tendency in Jesus that altogether matches his sharp awareness of scriptures while engaging in repartee with his challengers.

While we are in the subject of associating Jesus with all kinds of people including those of the educated class, it is well to draw from the work of Bargil Pixner, a Roman Catholic Priest/Scholar[28] who has researched an ancient document called the Protoevangelium Jacobi that has surprising things to say about Jesus and his background. The Protoevangelium is earlier than many documents that some scholars like to bring into play, (such as the Gospel of Thomas, which is often dated to around 250 AD, as they develop their notions about the pristine, original Jesus.

The fact that the Evangelium is a source known to the Roman Catholic Church should not, due to its early date, (about 150 AD) be confused with the

Middle Ages and the claimed authenticity of the bones of Saints and pieces of the real cross, etc.; this document is in the time frame of several of the respected and often quoted Apostolic Fathers, from whom Christians of many backgrounds draw effusively. A search of Google has uncovered some reservations about its authenticity, but it has a growing number of "hits", and is developing creative materials that help bring out its surprising conclusions.

The Protoevangelium Jacobi reports information provided by members of Jesus' family when the Gospel writer Luke interviewed them around 75 AD.[29] Among the findings are:

Mary, having family who were in the line of David, lived in a time when some women were given training in the law, and could serve in various ways in the temple. I have long felt that the Magnificat of Mary (Luke 1:46-55) must have had behind it a woman of some training and skill. Even though it echoed the Song of Hannah (I Samuel 2:1-10) in the Old Testament, Mary should not have been familiar with it, according to the suppositions being made about poor peasants and women. Her being in the line of David, along with Joseph, would indicate that the Magnificat (of Luke chapter 1) fits very well into the theme of God being active through Mary in the birth of the Messiah.

According to Pixner, "It seems that the evangelist Matthew had sources originating from Joseph's families at his disposal, whereas a Hebrew Haggadah dealing with the recollections of Mary came into the hands of Luke, probably on his visit to Jerusalem in the year 75 AD at the latest.[30] This agrees with a source other than Bargil Pixner;

According to Dr. Jim Fleming, there is an early Qumran Psalm that echoes Mary and Hannah from before 70 AD in the words: "My soul magnifies the Lord."[31] This adds extra force to Pixner's belief that the family of Jesus had an Essene background;

Jesus, who is often mentioned as a possible "third order Essene," was in a line of family who in fact were Essenes. They were not of the Qumran Essenes, but of the Jerusalem Essenes. Mary's birthplace was in an Essene area, where there was also a pool for ritual cleansing which was probably used by Jesus on the way to the Last Supper. This makes sense of Jesus' words in John 14 indicating that when someone has washed, only their feet remain unclean, as he and perhaps some of the

Disciples had to walk from the pool along dusty paths on the way to the supper.[32]

Judging from the Dead Sea Scrolls, the Essenes had scribes, as the scrolls found near the Dead Sea had to be put into writing and that writing was extensive.

Can't you just see Jesus, sometime after our "scribe" decided to take the challenge of becoming more deeply involved in spreading the news of the incoming rule of God's love, looking him in the eye and saying: "Every Scribe trained in the Kingdom is like a householder who takes out of his treasure what is new and what is old."?

It is not without relevance that Q contains no references at all to scribes. This could easily be explained by the fact that it was the producers of Q who were the scribes, whether their work was oral or written. So it would not be natural for such writers refer to the scribes in the "third person."

According to the Interpreters Bible, around the time of Jesus' birth the honorific title "rabbi" began to be given to scribes."[33] Though this does not absolutely nail down the argument about Jesus and the scribes, it certainly throws a lot of extra weight in that direction. One could even argue that as a Rabbi, Jesus himself was a scribe. A passage from Luke now shines with new meaning. (Luke 6:40).

"A student is not above his teacher, but everyone who is fully trained will be like his teacher." Since Jesus was such a fully aware student of the Old Testament, some of his students would have reflected that trait of Jesus. There are some who believe that Jeremiah's New Covenant as it appears in Jeremiah 31:31-34 pointed to a time when everyone will know the Lord. Knowing the Lord involves knowing the True Law, so the expectation is that everyone will be scribes. Jesus was surely aware of this. In Jeremiah 31:31-34, the New Testament/Covenant Law was to be written in people's hearts.

Matthew, the disciple of Jesus whose Hebrew name was probably Levi, was mentioned earlier as a possible Scribe. He was sitting in the Tax Office (Matthew 9:9) when Jesus called him. There is a strong possibility that Levi/Matthew, along with the un-named scribe who approached Jesus as a potential scribe were known, actual persons. This is mentioned due to the tendency to prefer "ghost" functionaries when pushing a theory, since their profile can be filled in "from scratch."

Judging from the fact that the Dead Sea Scrolls are written documents, the Essenes who produced them had scribes. Bargil Pixner, mentioned above, has tied Jesus' family to the Jerusalem Essenes, some of whom lived in the area where Jesus is believed to have observed the Last Supper. Some of the events of Holy Week are made more understandable by some items related to this; namely, that there have been pools uncovered, like the pools for ritual cleansing in the Qumran Community of the Dead Sea, which lies alongside the hills where the Essene scrolls were discovered. Jesus may have bathed in one of those pools in Jerusalem before the Lord's Supper. [34] This explains why he and the disciples still needed to be ritually clean with the foot-washing, having walked on a dusty path from the pool to the supper.

It is understandable that, due to the fact that the "oral transmission till 50 AD" theme has been so strong and has been assumed to be the only acceptable viewpoint for many, many years, that scholars and readers of the Bible in general would leap right over any suggestions to the contrary. But it is there, screaming to be heard! Why? Because the picture of Jesus being developed in our time needs to be challenged, and because truth is truth, no matter how long facts have been set aside or ignored.

As we recall Crossan's idea of learned people reviewing the Old Testament to make sense of Jesus' death, it could just as well have been scribes of Jesus who first of all, began to share the "Messianic Secret" of Jesus, and secondly, probed New Testament understandings that Jesus kept under wraps because of the tight security of the Romans and the danger of Jewish collaborators keeping the Romans informed of any "troublemakers."

According to the Interpreter's Bible, "Jesus teaching was itself a new law, which did not so much abrogate the old as "fill" it with the meaning God had intended it to have. It was important that a Christian should learn and understand this law, after the pattern of the earliest disciples, who were indeed *scribes trained for the Kingdom of Heaven.*[35]

5

JUDGE FOR YOURSELF

Just as scribes of the New Testament did, you can decide for yourself whether Jesus Christ deserves your trust. As you know by now, I believe that God is the loving and powerful God that Jesus proclaimed and that Jesus is the supreme interpreter of all scripture. This Jesus, who is greater than the Old Testament prophets, is the one in whom I trusted during the shock and sadness of losing our baby daughter so long ago. I have continued trusting Jesus throughout my life since then.

I have staked my entire life on this truth but not without having some of my most important questions answered. Even today, I continue to seek God's wisdom. I wrote this book because of my concern for people who are trying to solve faith intellectually but feel they have no one to ask. Some have been told they should not doubt but only believe. This is not very helpful to someone who has not yet *decided* whether or not to believe.

If you already believe but you have some questions that do not seem proper in church, do not be afraid to judge the claims of Jesus Christ for yourself. Some people are upset when any part of the Bible is questioned, believing that challenges

undermine the authority of God's Holy Word. But if
we do not ask the questions that are in our minds,
we run the risk of never growing in our faith. My
faith is strong, not simply because of my emotional
fervency. And certainly not because of my refusal to
entertain questions. Yet too many well-meaning
people have discouraged honest questions.

Regarding the Old Testament Scripture,
remember Jesus that *embodied the best and
transcended the rest.* I do not ask you to "just have
faith" without having some of your questions about
disturbing passages in the Old Testament answered.
I suggest that you familiarize yourself with the
words that Jesus spoke by reading the New
Testament first. Then when you go on to read the
rest, you will be able to look at all scripture through
the lens of what Jesus said about it. You will have a
much deeper and more accurate understanding that
is acceptable to your mind and satisfying to your
soul.

About Jim McClarey

Jim McClarey is always the first to credit others in his life for his successes; even so he has been recognized as a credible authority by both parishioners and peers. As a United Methodist minister, he served churches in several communities in Central Illinois for forty-five years. He was elected president of every Ministerial Association in the communities where he served until 1992 in Champaign where he chose instead to join Religious Leaders for Community Concerns. The roots of that decision go all the way back to childhood.

James Park McClarey (Jim) was born in Viola, Tennessee in 1933, the second of three children. Though he was too young to understand at the time, a delegation of the Ku Klux Klan entered the small church where his father James O McClarey was preaching and berated him for having allowed a black man to offer prayer during a service. They offered him a large sum of money in return for a promise never to let this happen again. James O refused the offer, and this fact is part of the heritage of the family. It affected Jim particularly deeply and may have been the basis for his lifelong interest in improving race relations.

While James O was oriented toward revival meetings, Jim's grandfather on his mother's side was a very scholarly pastor. Growing up with this double heritage, created a need to reconcile these divergent approaches in some way. In time, he made a serious study of the faith experience of both parents and some grandparents. Jim found reconciliation of contrasting realities to be a great part of his own faith.

Jim attended Blackburn College in Carlinville, Illinois as an art student in the early 1950s. Blackburn was (and is) one of the colleges that helped students earn their tuition through a campus work plan of fifteen hours a week. In 1953 tuition alone would have been half of his parents' income so the work plan made it possible for him to attend.

His major at Blackburn was art. He painted an eighteen foot wide mural called "The History of Blackburn" as a semester project. That mural hangs prominently in the Fine Arts Center at the college even today. There is a story about the mural that deserves a fuller treatment, but for that will have to wait for a future book. For now the efforts of Dr. John Comerford and his excellent staff at Blackburn are acknowledged with gratitude.

Jim's artistic talents extended to the written and spoken word as well. An English professor Dr. Alan

Walker was particularly impressed with Jim's poems. I grew up hearing Dad recite this poem not realizing that it was an original work, unpublished until now.

> "It is too late, I must go home. There is no inspiration here in this dark dreary office. Fate has dulled the mind which once could roam in darkness deftly without fear, and bring some thought of wonder home worthy of a laugh, a sigh, or tear. I must find rest, then early morn, where waters race and fishes play, and air, sky, sun and birds are blest shall be the secret hideaway where thoughts that fly as if by wings shall feast some soul on lofty things."

Dr. Walker was the first person in Jim's adult life to encourage his leadership skills along with his various forms of art; he opened the way for Jim and his friend Dean Jeanblanc to a Ralston Purina workshop in Michigan. While there they heard Barney Blakemore of the University of Chicago. He had never heard anything like it. At the time, the idea of asking questions about the Bible and feeling free to ask those questions opened a new door to him. This freedom to question his own beliefs was in time linked to his capacity to help people who had questions but often did not feel welcome in churches. They had been met with statements like: "Just believe: You can't think your way into Heaven."

Jim had a special feeling of empathy for people who had been hurt of confused by their churches. It was here he met the first agnostic he ever knew, and they developed a real friendship based on mutual respect.

So it was at Blackburn College that Jim had his first inclination that psychology and science as well as religious faith need to be seen hand in hand, not as competing elements. Years later, in a visit to Blackburn, he made sure to go by the office of his art teacher Dr. Harold Spencer. Remembering that he had said that Jim was the only one of his students who really wanted to remain an artist, and reminding him of that, Jim added that he was seeking his identity while exploring other areas. Very quickly Dr. Spencer asked: "Still seeking?"

Jim's quest to continue growing throughout life rather than think he had arrived started young and persists to this day. He always finds another book to read, another conversation to have, another viewpoint to consider.

Jim transferred to Illinois Wesleyan University his junior year and felt a call to Christian ministry during his senior year. Once while he was a student minister in a country church, a high school boy got up to sing a solo which contained the words: "My Lord is real, 'cause I can feel him in my soul." Jim recalls, as a student in seminary thinking that a person needs sound thinking and not just feeling. But as he continued to consider the opinions of all kinds of other people, he became more aware that God meets us where we are and helps us to where we can be.

During his first full-time appointment to the Methodist Church[36] of Forsyth, Illinois, Jim printed a Christian theology for young adults that contained in seed form several of his present day convictions about Christ and the Church, using self-drawn posters to illustrate the points. At first, the young adult group was shocked with the questions being voiced inside a church, but in the end, some of them had more questions than he did.

Later, while serving in Pekin Illinois, he became the first associate pastor ever to become President of the Pekin Ministerial Association. He became Vice President of the Pekin Human Relations Commission and sought to push a local industry to attract more black people from Peoria, in order to change the monochromatic complexion of the City of Pekin.

In Quincy, Illinois Jim formed a small group for study of Christian Theology in a Practical Way. This group, far from seeing theology as separate from practical living, began discussing the plans of the city to destroy twenty-five tons of government surplus food that had been stored underground. They interceded with the city and the Army Corps of Engineers to have the food shipped to the nation of Chad, which at the time was undergoing mass starvation. Within the Conference one fellow pastor criticized Jim for failing to approach starvation from a systemic point of view. Jim always says, "I am a "both/and" man, not an "either/or." Of course, he had concern for the larger problem of hunger, but some people were no doubt spared starvation by that shipment because he did not miss that opportunity.

While at Lincoln, Illinois Jim and his wife Kay journeyed to Dallas Texas, to get in on the ground floor of training to be leaders of the Disciple Bible Study Series, a four year program that covered the entire Bible, and then went more deeply into selected passages. They taught this curriculum together for several years and were amazed at the questions that poured forth as people read things that shocked their senses in the Old Testament. The radical differences with what they expected to see as Christians were quite disturbing to them. This greatly strengthened their belief that actual exploration of the Bible (and not just being satisfied to hear about it once a week in a sermon) is absolutely essential.

In Champaign Illinois, as pastor of First United Methodist, Jim participated in an interracial and ecumenical group, rather than joining the usual Ministerial Association. When a racist leader came to the Champaign-Urbana Area and made waves, Jim wrote an article for the local newspaper exposing what he felt to be dishonesty. He believed that he was acting in a small way with the courage his father had shown in Tennessee. He also accepted the invitation of a University of Illinois professor, to provide a paper based on Biblical principles to be taken to a meeting in the Near East on the question of the sharing of land and water between Israel and the Palestinians, and nearby nations. This was an exciting experience for Jim, and at least it may have helped some of the delegation to see the relevance of the Bible in a new way. Also, while in Champaign, he was invited to a radio station to discuss Biblical theology and enjoyed taking questions from listeners. That was well received, and it continued for about two years with brief talks on Christian faith on WCIA radio.

Through all the years, Jim continued to attend Biblical Seminars on a range of subjects. Three of these were led by members of the Jesus Seminar group, with whom he had some appreciation and some strong differences. He was especially drawn to the lectures of Dr. Jim Fleming, whom he first heard in Illinois, and later in a visit to the Holy Land in 1996. McClarey kept returning to hear more because he saw that Dr. Fleming had been able to interpret Jesus in terms of the land and the culture in which Jesus worked, more than any other person.

Jim attempted retirement in his early sixties, but did not last long. He began to accept short assignments to preach during pastors' vacations, and soon was filling in for more extended leaves of absence. He and Kay sold the home they bought to retire in and moved back into a parsonage (church-owned house) when he said yes to a two year interim pastor position. At last, when Jim was seventy-five years old they again purchased a house to retire in and he started in earnest to write his long-awaited book. But it was not to be a full-time pursuit because Jim served as a volunteer in the local church, led Bible study groups, and filled in for pastors by preaching occasionally. The United

Methodist Church of Woodstock, Illinois inducted him into their UMM Wall of Service in recognition of his service when he left there to move into his current residence in central Illinois.

In 2008, Jim's wife was diagnosed with cancer. Jim continued to write but slowed down the pace so that he could give most of his time and attention to her needs. Kay lived with cancer eight years, and he never left her side. She had always encouraged Jim to get the book done and had hoped to see it completed, but in October 2016 she passed on to her heavenly reward. Her last concern was to ensure that the chapel service she and Jim had established in their retirement community would outlive her. Indeed it did, and it continues today to provide ecumenical worship services on site with Jim still serving as a volunteer worship leader.

Jim writes in Judging Jesus chapter one that he was "a pastor who understands severe pain and loss" and that he "sat beside many hurting people." He has also *been* a hurting person, especially having said goodbye to his beloved wife Kay after fifty-nine years of marriage. With all of that, he is known among friends as an artistic man who appreciates humor and can tell a good joke. Jim loves to teach Bible lessons that engage the mind on many levels, including laughter. He often used the parable of the friend at midnight to teach that Jesus understood and used humor. Over the years Jim's students enjoyed his way of sharing this particular parable so much that he offers his notes on the lesson in the next section. He truly hopes that this book and the play will be a help to those who have tough questions about faith in God through Jesus Christ.

I want to introduce the humor of Jesus in its more philosophical side in a future book because it deserves a full discussion. However, I had an experience in several small groups that illustrated how very important the humor of Jesus was to the understanding of Jesus. I will share this short experience with you now in hopes that you, too, will find it refreshing and rewarding. Jesus' stories, which we call parables, were always lively, particularly in their original setting. The parable of the friend at midnight is an outstanding example of this.

The Parable of the Friend at Midnight
(Luke 11: 5-13)

If you have an opportunity in a sharing group of some kind, have someone read the story. After that, we will give some intriguing background that will explain why, when Jesus told the story, there were most probably peals of laughter on the part of Jesus' original hearers. Then we will set up a little Biblical drama.

I have arranged a mini-drama on the Friend at Midnight parable which is not only humorous but is fun and yet gets its point across in a surprising way. Every time I have used this mini-drama there have been peals of laughter. To build motivation, ask the group what kind of animals would a Jewish family at that time have in the pen. Inevitably, someone might say "Pigs!" Nope! No Pigs! Then ask people to volunteer to make the sound of one of the animals as the story is told. If no one or only a few people volunteer, you might say, "Herb, you'd make a good donkey!" Then give opportunity if needed, for people to practice the sounds. I once tried this on a group of fellow clergy, one of whom was Rev. Jack Travelstead, a Superintendent in the conference. I said "Jack, you'd make a good donkey! I'm telling this because Jack later said he had never heard this story in the light we had presented it.

I have seen pictures of ancient homes in Palestine in which there were two stories, especially when the homes were built into a hillside. The bottom part might be like a cave with a manger. Do you remember the birth of Jesus? The Inn may have been over a manger. There would have been a ladder to get the family up to their bedroom, where they all slept together. Before bedtime, the animals would be brought in for the night, for safety's sake, and a heavy door would be bolted shut. Then the family would climb up the ladder to the sleeping area. In the family's area downstairs there would be an earthen oven, perhaps a low table, and some baked containers of various sorts, and an oil lamp or lamps. It is obvious from the story that there was an oil lamp that had to be lit, and there was no electric switch. It would take a while to get an oil lamp going.

What kind of animals might be brought in for the night? You know some of the Bible stories and parables that included animals. Our list was the following: dog, sheep, a goat, chickens, hens, and a rooster. Now, which animal do you think would be awakened first? A dog or rooster would be early in the deal. You could arrange cue cards to guide the responses of the volunteers. I was pretty good at cackling, and this often brought laughter and helped people get started.

In a minute you can bring parts of the story before you again. Someone can play the parts of the husband and wife and the children, which should be speaking parts. Someone can be the baby and make crying sounds; another child can say: "Mommy, I'm scared!" Some of you are going to have to take the part of an animal….and don't be sheepish about it! It's not a put-down….in fact it takes talent to make animal sounds."

The person who is willing to knock on the door could say, "Hey, old buddy, wake up! I've had some company show up and I need three loaves to set before them!" The man wakes up grouchy: "Don't you 'old buddy me! Get lost! I'm with my wife and children in bed. This awakens the wife, who asks what is going on. Not pleased at all with his answer she could say, like; "What's the matter with his wife? Why doesn't she bake the bread? I know she has problems, but I do too!" Now the watch dog starts barking! The Rooster does his "cock a doodle do" confused that morning has come so early. The sheep begin bleating, the baby starts crying.

A narrator continues the story as it is told by Jesus, "But let me tell you, even if he won't get up because he's a friend, if you stand your ground, knocking and waking all the neighbors, he will finally get up and get you whatever you need."

The narrator says, "At this point, the man of the house says to himself something like this: I don't really want to give my friend the bread, but everybody is waking up any way, but if I don't the neighbors will all be awakened, and my name will be mud!"

Now, Jesus had a teaching point that went like this: If human beings, for less than perfect reasons, give help to someone in need, how much more will

God who is all loving, give good gifts to those who cry to him.

I hope this exercise will help you to make some of the parables come alive in your Bible study groups. Enjoy the humor Jesus offers!

NOTES

[1] Name changed to protect privacy.

[2] In this entire book, as noted on the copyright page, unless otherwise stated all scripture quotations are from the New Revised Standard Version Bible (NRSV), copyright © 1989 National Council of the Churches of Christ in the United States of America. Used by permission. All rights reserved worldwide. For more information, visit the website: http://bibles.org/index.php/licensing/

[3] The Jews of the "dispersion" were the people of the nation of Israel who had been scattered over the years when large powerful nations invaded Jerusalem and took people back to their countries to use them as slaves, sometimes highly skilled. Some Jews ventured into those areas on their own, but the word "dispersion" refers to all those displaced Israelites.

[4] Mark Twain, *Letters from the Earth* (Fawcett World Library 1968), 55.

[5] David Stern, Editor, *The Complete Jewish Bible* (Messianic Jewish Publishers, 6120 Day Long Lane, Clarksville MD 21029, www.messianicjewish.net, 1998), introduction. All rights reserved. Used by permission.

[6] Stern, *Complete Jewish Bible*, xli.

[7] Named changed to protect privacy.

[8] There are many examples women becoming a part of ancient Israel in the Old Testament; the most famous one is Ruth, the Moabite woman of the book of Ruth. The controversy around the issue of "foreign wives" is briefly explained in Nehemiah 13:23-27.

[9] Stern, *Complete Jewish Bible*, introduction.

[10] Luke 7:12-16 and John 11: 1-45

[11] Name changed to protect privacy.

[12] *The NRSV-NIV Parallel New Testament in Greek and English*, 1990, 512.

[13] I Thessalonians is an early writing, dated by some around 49 AD.

[14] J Stevenson Editor, *A New Eusebius: Documents Illustrating the History of the Church to AD 337* (Baker Publishing, Grand Rapids MI Revised 2013), 52.

[15] *Interpreter's Dictionary of the Bible Four Volume Set* (Abingdon Press New York 1962), 247.

[16] *Interpreter's Dictionary of the Bible*, there were "Scribes of the masses outside Jerusalem" (see also Matthew 7:29)

[17] John Dominic Crossan, *Jesus, a Revolutionary Biography* (Harper, San Francisco CA 1994), 146.

[18] Crossan, Jesus, *A Revolutionary Biography*, XII.

[19] John May, Editor, *The Oxford Bible Atlas Third*

Edition, Oxford University Press New York 1984), 109.

[20] May, Editor, *The Oxford Bible Atlas*, 112.

[21] Geza Vermes, *Jesus the Jew: A Historian's Reading of the Gospels* (MacMillan Publishers Co., Inc. 1973)

[22] Sepphoris was hidden from the awareness of scholars until its excavation in the last century. It was about four miles from Nazareth. Nazareth was probably during Jesus time a village of two to three hundred people, and thus not offering much for a highly trained artisan.

[23] *Interpreter's Dictionary of the Bible*, 246.

[24] *Interpreter's Dictionary of the Bible*, 246.

[25] *Interpreter's Dictionary of the Bible*, 247.

[26] *Interpreter's Dictionary of the Bible*, 247.

[27] J. Stevenson, Editor, *A New Eusebius: Documents Illustrating the History of the Church to AD 337* (Baker Publishing Group, Grand Rapids, MI 2013), 52.

[28] Bargil Pixner, *With Jesus in Jerusalem: His First and Last Days*, (Corazin Publishing, Rosh Pina, Israel 1996)

[29] Pixner, *With Jesus in Jerusalem,* 15-20.

[30] Pixner. *With Jesus in Jerusalem,* 19 Here Pixner reports that researchers in Israel, such as Professor Safrai and his daughter, were able to prove that

some kind of girls' service in the temple corresponds with historic facts. Such girls performed various services for the Priests and were given a thorough education in return. If this is true, it certainly has implications against those who describe Jesus as an unlettered peasant who could not read.

[31] From remarks made by Dr. James Fleming, at a live Jesus Seminar in Rochester, Illinois, October 22-24, 2006. For more information about Dr. Fleming and his lectures or workbook resources, visit his website at http://www.biblicalresources.net/about-biblical-resources.cfm.

[32] Pixner, *With Jesus in Jerusalem,* 66ff.

[33] *Interpreter's Dictionary of the Bible*, 247.

[34] Pixner, *With Jesus in Jerusalem*, 12.

[35] *The Interpreters Bible; Intro to Matthew*, 232.

[36] This was prior to the 1968 merger which created the United Methodist Church out of the former Methodist Church and the Evangelical United Brethren Church.

80540681R00070

Made in the USA
Lexington, KY
03 February 2018